KEEP YOUR PEOPLE
IN THE BOAT

KEEP YOUR PEOPLE IN THE BOAT

Workforce Engagement Lessons from the Sea

Crane Wood Stookey

Illustrated by Sydney Smith

ALIA
PRESS

Halifax

Cover design by Michael Atman, Spire Press Inc.,
www.spirepress.com, and Jessica von Handorf
Interior design and layout by Jessica von Handorf
Illustrations by Sydney Smith, www.sydneydraws.com

Also available in various ebook formats. For bulk purchases or
discounts, or for coaching or speaking services, contact
crane@cranestookey.com.

10% of the net proceeds from sales of this book go to support the
alternative education work of the Nova Scotia Sea School, a Canadian registered charity based in Halifax, Nova Scotia.

ISBN 978-0-9865588-1-8

ALĪA
PRESS

www.aliainstitute.org

I dedicate this book to my shipmates: the Tall Ship officers and crews I have had the honour to sail with, and the students and staff of the Nova Scotia Sea School, who have all been my teachers.

CONTENTS

LEADING ENGAGEMENT

W hat do the great "captains" of business, finance and industry have in common with the great captains of sailing ships?

They know how to get the best from their people.

How do they do this? You might think that a ship's captain will rely on the strength of their personality to keep their crew engaged by powerful command. Many do, but the best don't.

In my experience, leader-dependence is not good for performance. If people feel they can't do their best unless I "lead" them, *their* best is limited to *my* best, and they are unlikely to be fully engaged in their work because it's not *their* work, it's *my* work.

The question of how to lead people to a deep engagement is one I care deeply about. For the last 20 years I've worked to study and understand the ways that leadership can support people to be more engaged with their work and life. This book tells the stories of what I've learned during that time about engaging people to do their best and to be their best. In my years on sailing ships at sea and my years in organizations and businesses ashore, I have learned that I can engage people more completely when I treat them as complete people, with a bigger view than my immediate need for their work. I have found that this approach can bring extraordinary results. It also makes me feel happy to go to work.

This book isn't about "leadership" in the ways the term is often used: as visionary transformation of our collective future, courageous single-mindedness in overcoming opposition, or irresistible charisma that unifies everyone. Leadership has as many aspects as there are ways to influence people's thought and behaviour, but in the end all leadership is about engagement. Otherwise it's coercion, and coercion isn't leadership at all. The pursuit of engagement is the pursuit of a bigger view. When my view of the world and of my place in it expands, my engagement with it does too. This book is about how leaders can support people to reach their own most expansive engagement by taking the biggest view.

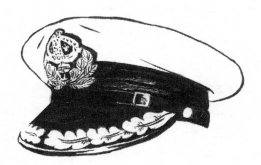

PART ONE—PRINCIPLES OF ENGAGEMENT

Chapter One |
Let Your People Grow

Life on a traditional sailing ship at sea is a strange mix of intense claustrophobia and vast space.

I have a choice. Which do I engage with?

My shipmates are generally not people of my own choosing, yet I am bound together with them in confined spaces for weeks at a time. The most irritating and unreasonable person on board may be the person I have to stand watch with. For my private quarters I get a bunk without enough headroom to sit up in, and on some boats, a curtain. If I have more gear than will fit on the narrow shelf or in the small sea chest, I sleep with it. I dress in front of my shipmates, or for privacy, lying down in my bunk. When there's wet weather for days at a time my clothes and bedding never dry out. In the summer it's hot and airless belowdecks, and in winter it's cold and dripping with condensation. And everything is always moving, sometimes creaking and swaying monotonously on smooth seas, sometimes groaning and tossing violently in a storm. It's like living in a washing machine on an endless cycle. I feel small-minded, self-protective and rigid, and I dream of jumping ship and getting as far from my shipmates and my job as I can.

At the same time, I'm out on the wide open sea. The big world reaches out to the horizon in all directions. The big sky arches over me. I see the sun rise and set, the moon wax and wane, and all the stars in the heavens. Colours and reflections glow on the waves in endless, amazing variety. I climb into the sky, far up into the rigging, to tend the sails. Life on a sailing ship at sea is about as big as it gets. I feel expansive and big-hearted, and delight in rolling with every wave. I feel full of love for this big, powerful ocean world, and I want the voyage to last forever.

What makes a great crew is being able to engage with the expansive state of mind even when things feel smallest.

———————————

One of the greatest crews I ever sailed with was on the square-topsail schooner *Californian*. I sailed on her for a season as Chief Mate (second in command), under Captain Andy Reay-Ellers, along the coast of California between San Diego and San Francisco. One of the jewels of this coast is the Channel Islands, particularly the more remote and northern islands, which are a national park. We anchored at these several times and sometimes took passengers ashore.

On one trip we anchored in Cuyler Cove on San Miguel Island. This is the most remote island of the chain, and is known for its fierce winds, rough seas and thick fog. It's also staggeringly beautiful, with an extraordinary density of wildlife. The day we were there was windy, blowing from the northwest, but the island sheltered us from the waves. We had been having trouble for a few days with the ship's anchor windlass, the hand-powered machinery that we used to haul the 500-pound anchor back up from the sea floor when we're leaving an anchorage. The windlass was old and tired and in need of an overhaul. It had a notched gear called a gypsy head that grabbed the anchor chain to pull it up, and this had been slipping. As we dropped the anchor at San Miguel Island the gypsy head finally stripped its clutch completely. That is, it broke. We wouldn't be able to use the windlass to get the anchor up, and would have to jury-rig a system with block and tackle, or a system of ropes and pulleys, to get it up by hand. We knew this would be a grueling chore when it came time to leave, but the island seemed well worth the effort.

At least there was no fog that day, and the cove was protected enough from waves that we could take passengers ashore using the launch with its outboard motor, making several trips. Captain Andy and I both wanted to see something of the island, so we took turns running the launch. Andy was bringing the last boatload of passengers back to the ship at the end of the afternoon when the outboard motor stopped as he was pulling up alongside. The wind immediately caught the launch and started to carry it away from the ship. This would have been only an annoying delay if Andy had been able to get the engine started again, but he pulled and pulled on the starter cord with no success. We tried to throw him a line but the launch had already drifted too far to reach him.

The wind was much too strong for Andy to row the launch back to the ship, and he and the five passengers began to drift quickly toward open water. They all were wearing life jackets and were in no immediate danger, but as they drifted farther from land they would eventually get into bigger waves and possibly swamp. They needed to be rescued. Captain Andy stood in the stern of the launch looking back at me on the ship. He hunched up his shoulders and lifted his arms in a question.

With Captain Andy in the launch, I was in command of the *Californian*, and I was scared. The failure of the anchor windlass meant we couldn't easily get the anchor up, turn on the engine and take the ship after them. It was the end of the day and the light was already starting to fade. We had to act quickly. The only thing I could think to do was to call the Coast Guard. They might be able to divert a fishing boat to help, or send a helicopter, or I didn't know what—but they would be able to handle it.

I told the crew what I thought. They were not impressed. A deckhand named Arnold, a man in his early twenties who alternated between sailing ships and driving trucks in Brazil, where his family was from, said he would go after the launch in the plastic kayak one of the passengers had brought aboard, and tow a line out to pull them back with. A young woman named Dora, about Arnold's age, immediately started getting all the spare lines of rope we had out of stowage in the lazarette.

I was against this idea. I didn't think we had enough spare line to reach them, I didn't know anything about Arnold's kayaking ability, or anything about kayaks in general, and it just felt like having one more person at risk out on the water. Drowning a crew member in a foolish kayaking stunt did not seem helpful. I felt my main responsibility was to be sure things didn't get any worse, and call for help. Heroics were not in my job description.

But Arnold and Dora countered all my arguments as they pressed on with getting ready. Arnold assured me that he had lots of kayaking experience in rougher water than this, and he was certainly very strong and fit. Fit enough that he could successfully paddle the light kayak back to the ship against the wind if the lines weren't long enough to reach the launch. He would tie the rope to himself, not the kayak, so that if anything did go wrong he would still be attached to the ship and we could recover him. Dora got others in the crew to help her lay out the lines on the deck, adding up the lengths and estimating the distance to the drifting launch, which she thought was still close enough.

Finally I recognized their confidence and their competence for what it was, and I surrendered my hesitation. Arnold launched himself off the stern of the ship in the kayak with his life jacket on and his line tied around him. The kayak landed nearly flat on the water, quickly stabilized and Arnold tore into the waves with his paddle, rushing after the launch with all his considerable strength. Dora tied the different lines together as fast as she could while I payed it all out over the ship's side after Arnold, making sure there were no kinks or snags.

I still didn't think we had enough line, but Dora remembered another coil we never used stowed in the forepeak and sent one of the other deckhands for it. The deckhand came running back with it just as the last line was starting to run through my hands. Dora tied the extra piece on and tied the end of it to the rail so we couldn't lose it, and Arnold pressed on the last 200 feet to the launch. Captain Andy had started rowing when he saw Arnold coming, not with any hope of getting closer to the ship, but at least to drift more slowly. I could see him throwing all his weight into the oars as Arnold got closer. One of the passengers leaned out over the bow of the launch and grabbed the handle on the bow of the kayak and pulled Arnold alongside, with only twenty feet of line left to us on the *Californian*'s deck. Arnold untied the line from his waist, leaned over from the kayak and tied it to the bow cleat on the launch. He'd done it.

With a cheer and huge sigh of relief I started hauling the line back onto the ship. Dora tailed on behind me with the other crew and some of the passengers. The line came dripping over the side and piled up on the deck as the launch drew closer through the waves. The passengers in the launch were all waving their arms and beaming at us. Our excited effort soon had the launch back alongside and the passengers started coming up the boarding ladder, elated and giddy. Captain Andy came up last. The crew and I hoisted the launch up the ship's side and secured it in its davits, and finally Arnold paddled alongside the boarding ladder and climbed up, pulling the kayak up behind him. Just to show how easy it all had been, he'd paddled himself back to the ship against the wind right beside the launch, and had been playing in the gusts behind the ship while the launch was hoisted.

Captain Andy congratulated me heartily for engaging the crew in such a successful recovery, and I had to explain that the credit really went to Dora and Arnold. The crew had engaged themselves, and had needed to work extra to engage me with them. My response to the crisis had been small, self-protective and rigid. Dora and Arnold's response had been big, creative and selfless. I didn't use these words to describe the situation to Andy, but that's how I described it to myself.

What can I say of myself about this incident? And what can I say of the crew?

For myself, this was an early voyage in my sailing ship career, and was a tremendously steep learning curve in many ways. I had been Chief Mate on another vessel the year before, but everything about that ship and her voyage had been more modest. The *Californian* and the coast of California were far more demanding, and repeatedly put me in over my depth. This made me feel cautious.

Was caution appropriate in this case? Was Dora and Arnold's kayak rescue just the lucky result of overconfident youthful exuberance, and my hesitation the mature, responsible perspective expected of the Mate?

In retrospect, no.

Arnold did indeed know kayaks, and knew his own ability. I didn't know either, and couldn't have been expected to. His easy return to the ship showed that his assessment of the danger was right. He also set up a safety precaution by tying the line to himself. He was never actually separated from the ship until it was clear he could handle it. Dora had a good sense of what lines we had readily available, and was a good judge of distance. I should have known more about our line situation, but the fact was, I didn't. In short, the crew was right, and I was wrong, and I learned a lot about what a strong, skilled kayaker can do.

On the other hand, I was the leader of an extraordinarily engaged and high-performing team, and I take some credit for that. Captain Andy and I had worked on this together, and we had formed a crew that didn't respond to a crisis with the helplessness of, "What do we do? What do we do?" We had built up a culture of initiative, trust and shared responsibility, a culture with a big view, and it was there to draw on even when my own view became tunnel vision. I trained the crew, and the crew in turn trained me.

A culture of the big view is not always the norm in sailing ship crews. Many captains create a culture of command and control that calls for strict hierarchy and places all the creativity and initiative in the hands of the officers. A ship in rough weather is not a place for consensus-building and decision-by-committee, but at the same time, in a storm at night, when the crew have to climb aloft to take down a sail that tore apart in the wind and is beating itself against the rigging with the sound of a machine gun, the situation is far too chaotic for one person to direct.

———————

How did Andy and I build a culture that encouraged a big state of mind in our crew?

We did it by accepting that leadership is a practice of generosity.

Here's an example. A basic maneuver of handling the ship is called "tacking." Tacking the ship is turning the ship in a particular way, toward the wind, and it requires the crew to handle all the sails in succession, in the right order, with the right timing, and in a hurry as the ship turns. The *Californian* is 145 feet long, her masts are 95 feet tall, and she carries 7,000 square feet of sail. Tacking her is a complex and demanding task.

Now let's say that I'm sailing under a different captain than Andy, someone old school who likes to see things done in the traditional way. He's respected for his ability and has had a long, successful career. We'll call him Captain Arrggh. When it's time to tack the ship, Captain Arrggh is at the wheel and he calls out, in a voice that carries to the masthead, "Ready About," which means get ready to tack. I repeat the command and then I start telling the crew, "You to the leeward headsail sheets, and you two to the windward. You to the staysail. You two, stand by the topsail braces." The vocabulary of the sea really is a language of its own, but don't worry about the salty lingo. I'm telling everyone exactly what to do.

Then when everyone's in position, I shout back to the Captain, "All ready on the foredeck," and he responds, "Helm's-a-lee," which is the command to tack.

The ship turns, and I have my eyes on the sails. At just the right moment, as the wind catches the sails, I call out to the crew, "Pass the flying jib, pass the jib," and the crew start hauling madly on the sails. Then at just the right moment, I shout, "Pass the staysail," and I wait, and then at just the right time I shout, "Let go and haul the topsail braces," and the topsail swings around. Then it's, "All hands to the foresail."

The ship is off on her new course, the tack is beautifully executed, and we've done a superb job, once again. Captain Arrggh believes that it all depends on his voice, and my voice. We've taught the crew to believe this too. They're all looking to us.

But sometimes, when the *Californian* is in different ports along the coast, we have passengers on board for a daysail. The deck is covered with landlubbers eating snacks and spilling their drinks. Having me jump up and start shouting commands over everyone's heads doesn't work so well. Captain Andy feels it's too intrusive. So let's let Captain Andy take command again now. He and I decide to try a different approach.

Captain Andy always wears a ball cap when he's sailing. He's back at the wheel charming the guests, because everyone wants to talk to the Captain, and in the middle of his conversation he turns his ball cap sideways so the bill is over his ear. The crew and I are also mingling with the guests, telling sea tales, but we all have half an eye on Captain Andy, and someone notices the turned ball cap. They excuse themselves from their conversation and move to a position at a sail. Another crew member notices them moving, and they move too. Quickly this awareness ripples through the whole crew, and everyone has moved into position. I'm standing up on the hatch and I give the thumbs up signal to Captain Andy, and he turns his ball cap backwards. The ship starts to turn, and now it's the crew who have their eyes on the sails. At just the right moment, as the wind catches the sails, they pass the flying jib, and pass the jib. At just the right moment, they pass the staysail. They let go and haul the topsail braces, and the topsail swings around. They all move to the foresail. The ship is off on her new course, the tack is beautifully executed once again and I have said...nothing. Not a word. No one has said a word. Nothing needs to be said.

The crew have tacked the ship dozens of times. They know their job. Now maybe one time they're a bit too quick on the headsails and I need to tell them, "Hold that sail, hold it." But I don't say anything. My arm raised up with my fist clenched is the command for hold. Because the crew also have half an eye on me. They see my fist, and hold. Then at the right time, with a wave of my hand, I let them carry on.

And when we go back to our conversations with the guests, they say, "That was very smooth. We didn't even hear any commands. How did you know what to do?" we smile and say, "Many hands. One mind. When we're all in sync, the ship tacks herself."

For Captain Andy and me, tacking the *Californian* in silence was our version of success: a crew so in sync with each other and with their work that the task could be accomplished with almost no word from us. Such synchronicity represents an expansive level of engagement.

The key to this culture of engagement we created was being aware of all the things we gave when we gave command.

When Captain Arrggh and I shouted out orders in the traditional way, we gave the crew clarity, precision and success at tacking. These are useful gifts, and the crew appreciated them. We also gave the crew dependence: they didn't do anything unless we told them to. We gave them a lack of trust: we implied that they couldn't do it on their own. And we gave them tunnel vision: we didn't expect them to pay attention to the big picture, but just to pay attention to us.

In sum, we gave them a small view of the task. Smallness is a place where people can hide. If all anyone has to do is follow our directions, they never really have to take responsibility or in any way show up fully themselves.

When Captain Andy and I let the ball cap give commands, we still gave clarity, precision and success at tacking. We also gave shared responsibility, mutual trust, and the ability to pay attention to the task and at the same time be aware of the big picture. In giving these things, we gave an expansive view of the task, and we took away any place to hide. In that storm at night, with this level of genuine shared responsibility people have no choice but to step up.

These are the gifts the crew need most if we want them to become deeply engaged and highly performing. These are the generous gifts, and this is the approach that makes effective leadership a practice of generosity.

———————

Generosity? Isn't leadership about getting people to do what you want?

No, it's not. Leadership is about getting people to do what *they* want. Leadership creates the conditions that support people to grow and prosper. Then our organizations, and our society, can grow and prosper with them.

This is what we human beings want most: to grow. We want to discover the best in ourselves. We want to prosper, and not just on a financial level. We want to accumulate experience, skill, wisdom, love and friendship, worthiness, usefulness and joy, and we want to define for ourselves what each of these means. We want to grow and prosper on our own terms.

This is particularly true of the post-Boomer generations. The paycheck and the corporate ladder are no longer enough. Learning and discovery are the prime motivators of the X and Y generations.

This sort of growth is a deeply personal thing. People who are engaged with something on a following orders level don't develop a depth of personal commitment. If we want to engage others, we can create conditions that support them to grow and prosper, on their own terms.

The reason leadership is a matter of creating the *conditions* for growth is that we can't do anything directly to make people grow. Marge Simpson, on *The Simpsons* TV show, is famous for saying, "People who say you can't change people are just quitters." But anyone who has tried to get a teenager to appreciate authority, or tried to get a politician to take a long-term view, knows that we can't change a person's outlook by telling them to change their outlook, any more than we can stand over a plant and say "Grow!" We can only take an indirect route by offering soil, water and sunlight. Then we have to let the plant do its own growing.

I experienced the power of the indirect route on a few memorable occasions as a child. I was a loser at team sports, and hated anything that made me wet or cold or uncomfortable. My parents exhorted me to "overcome my fears" and to "get over myself," but no one could ever tell me how to actually do that. "Be brave" wasn't useful instruction. Feeling guilty about not being brave didn't help either.

Then one year the Boy Scouts gave me a chance to discover that I could go winter camping and not dissolve into helplessness if my feet were cold. That summer my oldest brother David took me sailing on a day so windy the sailing race was cancelled, and he gave me the chance to discover that I could be scared and wet and tired and still keep control of the boat. It wasn't that the Boy Scouts or my brother gave me the toughness or confidence that I didn't have. I had those qualities already. They were just submerged. All I needed was the chance to discover them for myself.

My scout leader couldn't teach me toughness directly, but he could offer me winter camping as a sort of mirror in which I could see the bigger view of my own toughness. My brother couldn't teach me confidence directly, but he could offer me a windy day of sailing as a sort of mirror in which I could see the bigger view of my own confidence.

The camping and the sailing were far better teachers than the scout leader or my brother could ever be. But David and the scout leader created the conditions for me to encounter those teachers. They created the conditions for me to look in the mirror of my experience and discover the toughness that was already there, just submerged. I had to do my own looking and make my own discovery, but without the conditions they created for me I would have had nothing to look at.

When Dora and Arnold and the rest of the crew tacked the ship without direction, the ship became a sort of mirror in which they could see the bigger view of their independence, their competence and trustworthiness that, even if submerged, were already there. Andy's and my silence created the necessary conditions for the crew's discovery. This was our leadership. And it paid off big time when it was needed most, in a crisis where the crew's independence, competence and trust rescued the drifting launch.

Engagement is a state of mind. The fruit of generous leadership is an engaged and effective state of mind, a big view, in the people we lead. The generous approach to leadership is not about psychology, or charisma, or cheerleading, or indoctrination, which are common approaches but less effective in the end. The generous approach asks us to try to understand and foster what it takes for Dora and Arnold to enter a crisis with an assertive, creative and confident state of mind, rather than a state of mind that is caught in the smallness of "Help, help. What do we do?"

A generous leader has a lot in common with a good teacher. Both aspire to help people grow, to help people move from small to big. The leader's refrain, like the teacher's refrain, is this: "Let your people grow."

W hat are the conditions that foster a culture with a big view? What kind of leadership do you need to create them?

The Chinese philosopher Lao Tzu summed this up more than 2,000 years ago when he wrote:

The bad leader is hated and feared.
The good leader is loved and praised.
The great leader, when their work is done,
The people say, "We did this ourselves." [1]

This was our aspiration on the *Californian*, and I have experienced the remarkable power of this approach over and over again.

I once sailed with a young woman named Stephanie on the brigantine *Corwith Cramer*. The *Cramer* is a modern steel sailing research vessel operated by the Sea Education Society in Woods Hole, Massachusetts. She takes students from a variety of universities to sea for semesters of oceanographic science and seamanship training as part of their undergraduate degrees.

---

1. This well-known quotation is from Chapter 17 of the *Tao Te Ching* by Lao Tzu. The four lines have been rendered in English in various ways, and do not correspond to four lines of the original text, but are a simplification of the 11 lines of the original chapter.

We sailed from Key West on a two-month voyage to the Dominican Republic, the Cayman Islands and back to Key West, taking a somewhat circuitous route to collect scientific marine samples for the students' various experiments. We collected samples several times a day, looking for the extent and condition of Sargasso seaweed (the Sargasso Sea is vanishing), the distribution of plastic debris, changes in water quality at different depths, and so on. We anchored on Silver Bank, which is 70 miles off the north coast of the Dominican Republic but only 60 feet deep. It's where the humpback whales come to breed. We lowered a hydrophone over the side with a speaker on deck and listened to the songs of the whales all night. In the morning one of the whales followed close behind the ship for several miles as we sailed away.

There were about 18 student crew on the ship, divided into three watches. At sea the watches rotated being on duty for four hours at a time, around the clock. Half of each watch was on duty in the lab with one of the scientists, the other half, three students, was on duty on deck, sailing and navigating the ship with the officer of the watch. If we needed more hands to change sails, tack the ship or for some other maneuver we could call out the crew in the lab for a little while, but this 134-foot, 280-ton ship was operated most of the time by one professional and three students. People had to be pretty engaged.

As the weeks progressed the student crew became more and more proficient as sailors, and in the last month they started taking turns being officer of the watch in training themselves.

Late in the voyage we were off Miami before heading south to Key West. Near a city as big as Miami we expected to find increased concentrations of discarded plastic in the water column so we were taking some time to collect samples. Stephanie was the student officer of the watch, under my supervision. It was night and Captain Deborah Hayes had drawn a square on the chart, told Stephanie to keep the ship within that square, and gone to bed. To stay within the square, we had to do a good deal of maneuvering.

One might have expected Stephanie, relishing her new competence and trying hard to fill the role of ship's officer, to have been keeping close track and control over every action of her small crew, directing us to be sure everything went perfectly. This might be the way of Lao Tzu's "good leader," wanting to be praised for her "leadership." But when it came time to tack the ship, she called the other crew out of the lab, gathered us all together and said simply, with an excited smile, "Places, everyone."

The delight of the rest of the crew was palpable. Everyone suddenly realized that they, a handful of university science students, knew exactly what to do to tack this massive ship and could be trusted completely to do it. Everyone headed off to a sail, with Stephanie's excited smile shining on their faces too.

Stephanie didn't make the tack about *her*. She made it about the crew. She was obviously excited about being able to trust them, which of course made them want to be trustworthy. We maneuvered beautifully and tirelessly inside our box through the night.

I also aspire to be the leader that Lao Tzu describes, to make my leadership not about me. While I feel I have developed a strong understanding of how to do this, generous leadership is hard to give. I often find that in the pressure of the moment, in the rush to get things done or under the weight of my responsibility, I forget, and I fall back into the small, fearful, controlling view of making it all about me. But when I succeed in leading generously, the results always exceed my expectations.

At the Nova Scotia Sea School, the sail-training organization I founded in Lunenburg, Nova Scotia, we build our own wooden boats and go on sailing expeditions along the coast, taking advantage of the Maritime traditions to help young people learn to grow up well. We also run professional development programs for educators and trainers, and offer adult and corporate team-building programs.

The expedition boats we build are 30-foot open boats. Crews of 10 teenagers—many of whom have never been in a boat before—sail these boats on voyages among the islands of the Nova Scotia South Shore, on trips lasting anywhere from five days to three weeks. The crews learn to take command of the boat, and of their lives. The boats have no engines, no cabins, no electronics. They have two masts with sails (a spritsail ketch rig), and eight 13-foot oars. When there's no wind, the crew rowing with the oars are the engine. We anchor at night in protected coves, but we live in the boat, cooking and sleeping under a tarp stretched between the masts.

The goal of the instructors is to teach ourselves out of a job as quickly as we can. Just as on the *Corwith Cramer*, we try to hand responsibility to the student crew as much as possible.

On one 10-day voyage a young woman named Zoë was my assistant instructor. There were also two senior crew, veterans of previous voyages, who were sailing as Leading Crew, instructors-in-training. After a few days I turned command of the boat over to the three of them for the day. I went and lay down in the middle of the boat along one of the midship thwarts, the rowing benches that run across the boat, and rested my head on the gunwale. After a while I folded my hands on my stomach and pulled my broad-brimmed straw hat down over my face.

I didn't really sleep. We had a long, vigorous beat to windward, the kind of sailing that calls for careful attention from the crew steering at the helm. I could tell by the motion of the boat and the sound of the wind in the sails whether we were badly off course or sailing poorly. For a while I made a comment or two from under my hat when the crew steering at the helm veered too far from the wind, but then I stopped. Zoë and the Leading Crew kept the steering focused, or they got distracted themselves by the thrill of the ride, then focused again, and we made good progress.

I lay there under my hat for a couple of hours, keeping still even through the commotion of tacking the boat, listening and feeling everything, enjoying the conversations and excitement of the crew. I dozed occasionally, waking up whenever the motion of the boat changed. But the crew did well, and I just lay there.

At the end of the trip Zoë and the two Leading Crew told me that they had been so pleased to see me sleeping while they took command of the boat. It made them feel their responsibility was real. They felt trustworthy and competent, eager to rise to the task. At the same time they knew I hadn't abandoned them. One of the Leading Crew told me that having me sleeping there through the maneuvers made him feel safe.

When the people say, "We did this ourselves," it's not that they have become leaderless. It's that the work has become about them, not about the leader.

If we try to engage people on our terms, that's coercion, the "bad leader" Lao Tzu described. We can try to engage people on shared terms with our charisma, clarity and inspiration. That's the "good leader," but this leadership creates dependence and a narrow kind of followership. Anyway, we don't all have charisma, and even the charismatic among us have off days. The way to create a culture with the resilience of the big view is by supporting people to engage themselves, on their own terms. When they say, "We did this ourselves," they are inspired to keep doing it, better and better, because it's theirs.

Practicing this sort of leadership can be scary. If we are really generous and trusting enough to step back and let people do it themselves, where's the control? Do we let the crew run the ship? Well, yes. If our goal is to engage them as fully as possible, that's exactly what we do. There will be limits, but to the extent that they can, the crew run the ship. That's the point.

There will be other factors besides engagement that may bear on this question of people doing it themselves. On large-scale divisive questions like the role of government or raising taxes people can be so deeply engaged with their own side of the debate that their engagement becomes entrenchment, and the only way forward is for a strong leader to force the issue.

I accept that this is true, and I don't propose that the generous leadership approach is the only effective leadership style. Leaders do well to be skilled in various leadership styles, and much has been written about the diversity of approaches. The generous leadership that I espouse is specifically about the techniques and benefits of practicing leadership in terms of engagement.

I would also say that the effects of engagement are scalable. The success of such historic leaders as Martin Luther King, Mahatma Gandhi and Nelson Mandela are in large part due to their extraordinary ability to engage people. Engagement builds capacity and this takes time, but once an expansive engagement takes root it can have the capacity to change the world.

Forceful leadership tends to be in a hurry. Even when it achieves its goals, it has trouble achieving engagement, and this makes it hard to sustain. "Urgency destroys capacity." [2]

---

2. Meg Wheatley, author of *Leadership and the New Science* and numerous other leadership and business books, in a lecture at the ALIA Institute Summer Program, Halifax, Nova Scotia, Summer 2009.

Ask any child if they feel deeply engaged by their school, and what do most answer? Ask any child how their school should be run, and they'll have plenty to say.

There's one school that actually listens. It's the Sudbury Valley School, a private school for all grades in Massachusetts. It's an extreme example of supporting people to do it themselves, but it fosters a truly remarkable level of engagement in its students. We'll come ashore for a while, and visit this school.

Sudbury Valley calls itself a democratic school, which is accurate, because all decisions regarding the day-to-day operation of the school are made by the weekly School Meeting. Every student, in all the grades, and all staff have a vote in the School Meeting. The staff have a lot of influence and are respected as elders, but there are more than 200 students and around 11 staff, so the students rule. The School Meeting sets the budget, allocates funds, creates and enforces the rules, and hires and fires the staff.

That's right. The students run the facility, hire and fire the teachers, and set salaries. When I visited the school, a group of students had recently decided that the leather and craft room, outfitted in the 70's, wasn't used enough, and more people now wanted to learn about music recording. So they petitioned the School Meeting to include money in the next budget to turn the room into a recording studio, and hire a part-time recording-tech teacher. They had to deal with the Parents Association to raise the funds, and convince both Meeting and Association that this, rather than competing projects, was the place to spend the money. They then found a teacher and petitioned the Weekly Meeting to hire them. They designed the studio together with the teacher, and purchased and installed the equipment, within the budget.

When I was there several students were recording together, and the studio was booked weeks in advance. Students oversaw the booking. There is no tenure at Sudbury Valley, so the tech teacher's contract is renewed annually by the School Meeting. Or not.

The students, at all ages, create their own curriculum. They learn what they want, when they want. They decide when they're ready to graduate. To get their high school diploma, they must convince the School Meeting that they are ready to enter the larger world as effective, useful adults. They must show ample evidence of learning, responsibility and action over the years to support their case.

But this is incredible. How can this be? If the students run the school and do what they want, don't they all just run amok? When I visited the school, I was able to attend the weekly Judicial Committee meeting, which has one staff representative and a student representative from each of the school age groups, including elementary. There is a box in the living room of the school with forms anyone can use to write up complaints about infractions of the rules.

The first two cases heard by the Judicial Committee on the day I was there were of students who had written themselves up. One had been roughhousing with a friend and broken a lamp. Another had misused school property. They turned themselves in. The Committee heard the cases, gave punishment of limited use of certain facilities for a period of time, and required practical restitution.

The last case the Committee heard that day was for a boy who had been a behavioural problem in the school for months. He had recently been warned that his behaviour might lead to expulsion. He was in the school building but refused to appear before the Committee. After deliberation, the Committee expelled him. They didn't really have a choice. The policies, set by the School Meeting, were clear. The infractions had accumulated, the warnings had been given, and so the students did what they had to do. They expelled one of their own.

This is about as far at the other end of the spectrum from standardized testing as you can get, and it's not for everyone. Some people need more structure. But the results of this approach at Sudbury Valley are impressive. The school is a 40-year-old success: financially sound (it costs less to put a child through this school than to put them through the public system in the same town), a waiting list for admission, students who decide to go on to university generally getting into their first choice school, [3] and a raft of other schools around the world based on the Sudbury Valley model.

Most important, its success shows in the students. You will not find a more engaged student body anywhere. They take the initiative for their own work, they innovate when needed, they take personal responsibility for the welfare of their organization, and they hold each other accountable. It's a manager's dream come true. Some people may have a problem with the style of education, which is like saying some may not want to buy the product, but with people lined up to get in, the school has all the market share it can handle. What's not to like?

---

3. *Legacy of Trust: Life After the Sudbury Valley School Experience* by Daniel Greenberg, Sudbury Valley School Press, Framingham, Massachusetts, 1992.

The Sudbury Valley School is an extreme example of people engaging themselves on their own terms. While the school is very effective in creating a culture of deep engagement, this approach would be overreaching for many organizations. Nevertheless, if this degree of trust and generosity can produce such remarkable results with children and teenagers, what could some degree of the same approach do for adults?

With some exceptions, like the expelled boy, people who are given genuine responsibility are likely to hold that responsibility in a trustworthy way. Similarly, people who don't feel trusted don't feel engaged. They are less inclined to be trustworthy, because they know it's not expected. As Lao Tzu said of the bad leader:

> They have no faith in their people,
> And their people become unfaithful to them. 4

Trusting people with real responsibility actually makes them more trustworthy.

In my coaching and training work, I often find that while leaders may think these ideas sound great, they're inclined to say, "But it wouldn't work with *our* people." This resistance to generous leadership is common, but it isn't really about "our people." It's more about our own egos. Much as we like to think otherwise, it's rarely true that "they are the problem and I am the solution." It's really about the fact that trusting the

4. *Tao Te Ching* by Lao Tzu, Chapter 17.

collective competence and being generous with responsibility can leave us feeling as if we're giving up our leadership rather than taking it on. We all want to be loved and praised, leading the charge with our gleaming sword held high. Right? If we're not prominently rallying the troops, how will everyone know that we're indispensable? How will we know it ourselves? Isn't this whole power-to-the-people approach just an invitation for someone to ask, "So what are we paying *you* for?"

This brings us to that out-of-place, out-of-favour word, "command." Most leaders today know that command-and-control is out, bad form, Neanderthal. We're all supposed to be Captain Andy, not Captain Arrggh, even though Captain Arrggh seems much more captainlike than Captain Andy, who doesn't seem to do much. But this is a misunderstanding. Command doesn't deserve the bad rap it's been getting. Being a generous leader is still very much about command.

The English word "command" was originally synonymous with "commend," as in "I commend to your care," or "I commend your courage." So "command" has the sense of entrusting, and of praising what is worthy. Its root comes from two Latin words, "*man*" which means "hand," and "*dare*" which means "to give." It shares this root with "mandate," and "*co-*" adds a sense of working together. The commander holds the mandate, and also gives it. So "command" means to give a mandate into worthy hands, to entrust a duty to a worthy person.

What this implies is a leader whose mastery of the situation creates a culture in which everyone involved feels fully worthy of holding the shared mandate. Being the person who creates the conditions for everyone to step up and do it themselves is a huge responsibility. Ensuring that this kind of generosity is maintained through all levels of an organization to the point that it becomes a cultural norm requires very strong leadership. It's just not loud, directive, "I'm the most important person here" leadership. That makes us look big, but it makes others feel small and think small. Instead, it's "You're the most important person here" leadership. That may not make us sound so important, but it allows others to think big.

The Sudbury Valley School was founded by Daniel and Hanna Greenburg, who are still there. They are part of the staff, and they quietly serve as elders and protectors. Visiting the school, you might not notice them. As you spend more time there, their presence would be felt more and more. They are powerful holders of the mandate of the organization, and in many subtle, perceptive ways they continually give and re-give that mandate to the students and staff, reinforcing the worthiness of everyone. They still hold the power of conviction that founded the school in the first place, and they inexhaustibly spread that power as if by osmosis.

When I was "sleeping" on the Sea School boat, I can say that my presence pervaded the boat in a powerful and beneficial way. It had taken me a lot of work to get the crew to the point where I could step back to that extent, an effort I have to make again and again with every new crew on every voyage. Being able to step back is successful command: stepping back from being the capital-L Leader, and instead focusing on creating the conditions that allow people to have a big view of what they can accomplish, so they can say, "We did this ourselves."

When the Sea School builds one of our expedition boats, we get the wood from an eco-forestry woodlot in New Germany, Nova Scotia, that's been producing a steady supply of lumber for more than 150 years. Its current owners, Jim and Margaret Drescher, run the business on the premise that their true product is the forest itself. Lumber is a byproduct. Because they and the generations that have preceded them have viewed the forest as the product, there is now, after continuous lumber production that has supported several local families for 150 years, more potential lumber growing in the trees of the forest than there was when the first tree was cut. The true source of wealth is not the lumber, it's the forest.

The true source of wealth in an organization is not its products, but people's ability to produce those products. Of course, right? But we can see this idea in much more personal terms. Organizational strength is the inseparable byproduct of personal strength. It's not enough that people have good health benefits, free day care or a pool table in the office. It's not even enough that people have trust, real responsibility and a big view. It's only enough if these things create a culture that fosters personal growth: self-discovery, self-awareness, self-appreciation. Organizational strength is a very personal matter.

At the same time, people's self-discovery is entirely their own business. As I said, we can't make people grow. "Grow there, you workforce!" Not really. Once again we take the indirect route of creating favourable conditions, and allowing those conditions to support whatever growth is possible.

We trust the indirect route because we trust that what an organization needs from its workforce is already there. What you need from your people is already there. It may be submerged, but it's already there.

This doesn't mean that everyone has submerged accounting skills waiting to blossom under your generous leadership. It means that your finance staff has more precision, creativity, perceptiveness of future trends, and insight into the creation of wealth than you, or they themselves, are likely giving them credit for. Not just your CFO, but your finance staff. Or your warehouse staff. Warehouse staff would have different submerged qualities, like insight into efficiency, or how to make an inherently repetitive and menial job worth taking responsibility for.

How do all these people's various qualities surface? Here I'd like to introduce a metaphor that I touched on in the first chapter, the metaphor of the mirror. When we look in a mirror, we see ourselves. We interact with ourselves. A mirror is a tool of self-discovery, self-awareness, self-appreciation. The most generous leadership of all lies in offering a work experience that is mirrorlike, that shows us not just something about our professionalism, but also something about who we really are as people. As leaders we can't tell people what to see in the mirror. But we can conceive of our organizations as places that support people to see and engage themselves on their own terms, at a deeply personal level, at work.

Each of the stories I've told are about situations that have this mirrorlike quality, situations where the people involved see themselves in a fresh and freshly appreciative light. Exactly what each person saw probably ranged across a broad spectrum. Who knows what each person saw?

And who cares? Self-discovery as part of people's work experience is the ultimate in engagement, but the specifics of it are irrelevant to us as leaders. What people see of themselves in the mirror is entirely their own business. We can't possibly see what they see anyway. What matters is that people whose work experience enriches their self-understanding as much as it enriches their bank account come to work with a sense of gratitude and delight, eager for more. And because they are seeing this in the mirror of their own experience they say, "We did this ourselves." When the launch is drifting away, they see themselves as the kind of people who can step up and save the day. What more engagement can we ask for?

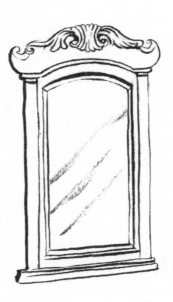

As I noted earlier, this kind of work experience is particularly important for younger employees today. Gen X and the Millennials are likely to put their self-interest ahead of their employer's interests, in the sense that they value meaning, balance and learning over traditional career advancement and the 60-hour work week. To keep these young people, or have them be attracted to your business in the first place, offer them a mirrorlike workplace where they can learn something about themselves. Self-awareness is the new definition of success.

The workplace holds up its mirror for us as leaders too. When I couldn't see the possibility of rescuing Captain Andy in the drifting launch it was because I, the leader, couldn't see that possibility in myself. The crew's response was a wonderfully vivid mirror in which I could see my own fear and hesitation. I saw a lot that day about my self-imposed limitations. I also saw how essential it was that my generosity and trust had engaged the crew so deeply in their work. In that moment of crisis, my leadership was inadequate to save the launch. In that moment of crisis, my leadership was responsible for the strength that saved the launch.

When people say, "We did this ourselves," the situation becomes leaderproof. That is, success doesn't depend on the top of the pyramid. That top is not the seat of the Pharaohs. It's a small, pointy, uncomfortable, precarious, lonely place. It's a ridiculous place to sit really, a place where adequate information has a hard time reaching, but where every weakness and uncertainty is magnified a hundredfold and cascades down on everybody. We really don't need to sit there. "It's not about me."

Leaderproof leadership isn't a denigration of leaders. It's an attitude of leadership that puts leadership in its proper place, a step or two back. We can all fall into the pattern of trying to be the capital-L Leader, the great man or woman on whom everything depends, but we can be more generous than that. Along with "Let your people grow," we can also remind ourselves, "It's not about me."

Chapter Three |
Don't Paint the Rocks

H ow does a leader make their leadership leaderproof?

Let's rejoin a voyage with the Nova Scotia Sea School.

The Sea School boats have no place set aside for the crew to sleep. There are no bunks. When night comes, we lie down together and sleep on the oars.

Have you ever slept on a set of oars? No? Really never? Well this is how it works.

To go to bed, once the tarp is set up between the masts, first we get what we need for the night out of our duffel bags: foul weather gear and boots in case of a storm, warm clothes to wear during our turn on night watch, sleeping bags. Then we stow our duffel bags down under the thwarts, the rowing benches that run at intervals across the boat. To make a place to sleep we take the 13-foot oars and lay them side by side, spanning the gaps between the rowing benches. All the oars lying together next to each other make a kind of platform, and we lie down across them to sleep. They're hard and uncomfortable, so for comfort everyone gets a half-length foam pad, a quarter of an inch thick. Once the oars are in place we spread out our sleeping bags. Now we're lying on the oars over the duffel bags below so we can't get at the duffel bags anymore. If anyone forgets something we all get up so we can shift the oars and get at the duffel bags again. If in the morning one person won't get up, we can't shift the oars so none of us can get at our duffel bags to dress.

The power of the situation is that the instructors never have to say, "Okay, crew, it's time to practice our teamwork. So you're all going to do this really fun team-building exercise we made up." And the crew replies, "Forget your stupid game. What do you know?"

All we have to say is "Time to go to bed." The oars do the rest, and they do it much more effectively than we ever could. Our telling the crew to work together is just hot air. The oars are real, and they focus, involve and commit the crew in a very real way. It doesn't matter how people react to the sleeping arrangements: if they want to go to bed they have to deal with it.

If the crew are having a hard time with each other, bickering and complaining, usually the voice of calm and collaboration is already present in some member of the crew. If the instructors trust that and are patient, that person can discover their own leadership and let it surface. If the instructors aren't patient—if we step in to be "helpful"—we dilute the situation with our leadership. Everyone looks to us instead of to themselves, all the power of the situation leaks out, and the person who was about to discover that they are big enough to be the voice of gentleness and cooperation retires quietly back into their smallness.

Now at first the crew are likely to be saying to the instructors, "Tell Joe to get his act together. He's holding everything up. Why don't you tell him? What do they pay you for, anyway?"

But our leadership, our command, consists of entrusting the duty of engagement to the oars. The oars are worthy of the task, and we let them take command, recognizing that the oars will support the crew's discovery of cooperation better than our intervention ever could. Then when the crew needs to work together to sail the boat through rough water, avoiding the rocks and reefs, they've got the working together part down and can focus on the sailing. Sailing may be new to them, but because they can work and learn together they can more quickly acquire the skills to keep the boat safe.

We created the conditions that support people to discover their ability to work together when we designed the boat. It might have been possible to devise a system of panels that fold up into place at night to make individual beds, which could be folded down by each person if they needed to get at their gear again. But from the engagement point of view that would have been poor design. It would have been making up something extra for sleeping, and would have required us to make up something else extra for building engagement. The oars are already there. They're real, and they're hard to argue with. How can we use them for more than rowing in a way that will entrust the duty of fostering self-discovery to the oars, knowing that if we set it up right the oars can do a better job than we could? With a well-designed situation, the situation becomes leader-proof and does the work for us.

We had a rock tumbler when I was a teenager and I remember it vividly. We would find small rocks at the beach that we liked the look of, and put them in the metal can the tumbler came with, adding some special grit for them to tumble in. The can had a rubber lining to keep the noise down. We sealed the lid and put the can in the tumbling machine where it rested on little wheels turned by an electric motor. The wheels rotated the can so the rocks tumbled around inside. When we opened the can after it had slowly turned for several weeks in the basement, the rocks had polished themselves into gems. I kept some of those polished rocks for years and carried them in my pocket.

I've long felt the rock tumbler offers a helpful metaphor for considering what conditions can help people grow and prosper. We can look at the tumbler as having three conditions. It's *contained*. The rocks don't get out until they're done. There's *friction*. We actually add grit because friction is what does the work. And in the end we *discover* the natural brilliance of the rocks, which was there all along.

These three conditions are also useful to support people in their personal growth. First, we have a container; that is, we have a situation compelling enough to keep us involved long enough for some discovery to happen. A short-lived or leaky container, one we can easily get out of, doesn't cut it.

Then we have friction. We have something that wears away our sense of limitation, or our fixed ideas, or our stuck habits. This friction can be gritty and rough, like the challenge of climbing a mountain or crossing the ocean or sleeping on oars, but it doesn't have to be. Friction is simply anything that cuts through the ways that we're stuck. For someone stuck in antagonism and criticism, offering them a simple appreciative kindness can be very frictional. We could be rocked gently and lovingly in a pile of cushions if that's what's needed, and that could still be friction.

Last but not least, we have discovery. We discover the inherent brilliance of the rocks. Everyone has their own natural brilliance. It may be submerged but we trust that it's there, and that given favourable conditions it can be discovered.

But we have to be careful not to imagine that we know what other people should discover about themselves. When we use the rock tumbler metaphor at the Sea School we have a motto that goes with it. We say, "Don't paint the rocks." If we open a real rock tumbler after the rocks have been polished we might find a rock that didn't turn out quite the way we expected. We might look at it and say to ourselves, "This one's okay but it would be better if it were more like quartz. We'll paint it pink." But the point of the rock tumbler is that it brings out whatever natural brilliance the rocks already possess. It's not up to us to say what that should be. We can't turn a rock into quartz even if we want to, and painting it pink doesn't accomplish anything.

Similarly, when we apply the metaphor to working with people, we don't try to "paint" people with our own expectations. "Don't paint the rocks." Rather than try to manipulate people to be what we think they should be, we support them to shine in their own way. Then our organizations, and our society, can shine with them.

———————

Because we cannot create or direct self-discovery, our technique once again takes the indirect route. We focus on container and friction. Designing the Sea School boats so we sleep on the oars is a well-contained, well-frictioned situation. Adding "leadership" to it, by directing the crew when they're having trouble, pokes a hole in the container and lets the power of the friction leak out.

Ships and boats in general are great containers and there is much we can learn from them. Unless we're going to jump into the ocean and swim ashore, a ship can definitely hold us long enough for something to happen. But the ship contains us not just because we're at sea and can't get off. Every aspect of life at sea holds our attention and our participation. The schedule is repetitive and rigid. Every morning we polish the brass and scrub down the decks before breakfast. We're on duty for four hours in the daytime sailing the ship, then off duty for eight hours in which we eat and sleep, do chores and maintenance, then on duty sailing the ship again for four hours at night, and so on, around the clock.

Throughout this time, everything about the ship is giving us constant feedback. If we're not paying attention to our steering, the compass will show us. If we're not paying attention to how we trim the sails, the ship's speed will show us. If we're not careful with how we coil the lines, tie the knots, stow the gear, check the rigging, or any of myriad other details, then in that storm at night we'll be imperiled by snags of rope, jammed knots, gear flying loose as the ship rolls, broken rigging, and you can imagine what else.

It may be the Mate's job to draw our attention to these details, but the ship is really in command here. It's the ship that speaks the loudest, and gives the strongest, most inescapable feedback if we start to slack off. This is one of the main points about container. A well-made container gets people focused, involved and committed more effectively than we can focus, involve or commit them ourselves. With a well-made container, the situation is in charge, and it does the work for us.

There is considerable friction inherent in the shipboard container. The repetitive schedule, the power of the weather and the sea, the temperament of other members of the crew, the incessant demands of the ship, these are the things that wear down our attachment to personal territory, our resistance to working closely with people not of our own choosing, our need for entertainment. I spoke at the start of the book about the contrast at sea between intense claustrophobia and vast space. The claustrophobia can be frictional, as you can imagine, but the space can be frictional too. It wears away our smallness. When we climb aloft to work on the rigging, a hundred feet or more above the deck, we are literally climbing into the sky. The ship with all its constraints seems far away below us and our thoughts and feelings expand into space. There can be many ways that we get stuck in trying to protect ourselves from the demands of the situation at sea, by keeping ourselves small, but our defenses can dissolve out into the horizon, and the big view, the expansive state of mind, returns to us.

This is when discovery happens. It's usually not the small, claustrophobic part of our experience that is mirrorlike. It's the bigger, expansive experience that holds the mirror up for us and allows us to discover that we have more equanimity, more resilience, and a bigger point of view than we thought we did.

The power of this container approach goes beyond the outer physical circumstances of the situation we're in. Even the way we do things can have the three qualities of container, friction and discovery. Within the overall container of the *Californian*, the maneuver of tacking served as another, specific type of container. The crew can't just leak away in the middle of a tack and go to their bunks if they're having trouble. If they did, they would leave sails flogging themselves to shreds in the wind and a ship turning circles out of control or stopped dead in the water. And when the crew came back up from their bunks the situation would still be there facing them. The tack contains the crew's attention and participation.

When the crew under Captain Arrggh were stuck in their dependence on following detailed orders, Captain Andy and I got them unstuck by adding the friction of silence. At first the crew may have been resistant, wanting the comfort of commands. If we had said, after the first few less-than-excellent tacks, "Well, that doesn't work, we'll have to start telling everyone what to do again," the crew would have remained stuck. Trusting in the power of the maneuver to hold people, and in the power of our silence to wear out their dependence, we created the chance for the crew to discover their initiative, shared responsibility and big view.

Container practice is mostly a matter of paying attention to the ordinary circumstances of our situation with the point of view that every detail can be useful in helping us get unstuck. We don't say, "Now we tack the ship, later we'll do some teamwork development." We say, "Is there a particular way we can tack the ship that will also support people's personal growth?" We don't have to waste the opportunities that already surround us. The ship, the oars, the tacking, all these things can be more than just objects or tasks. They can also be mirrors.

Sadly, most of us don't have a ship. What if all we have is an office space where people wander out of the container for lunch and leave at the end of every day, where the copy machine and the computer network just don't have the same commanding quality as the oars?

No problem. Even that situation contains circumstances we can take advantage of to do some of the work for us. We'll come ashore again and visit an office that needs some help.

Alice worked in a company where her department had weekly all-team meetings. They were hellish occasions, thick with territoriality and blame, a regular weekly gut-shot to morale, creativity and effectiveness. They were also male-dominated and oppressively hierarchical, with an entrenched and fearful (and feared) leadership. Alice, in a new position at the bottom of the totem pole, hardly said anything, and what she did say was dismissed.

Alice really didn't want to get sucked into this culture, which everyone else seemed resigned to as the norm, but she felt powerless to address it. In an effort to introduce a little softness for herself into this inhospitable environment, she began bringing small flower arrangements to put on her desk. Then one week, she took her flowers and put them on the side table against the wall in the meeting room before people came in. When the meeting started a few people commented on the flowers, some surprised, some cynical, and the meeting proceeded as usual. Alice brought flowers for several more weeks, and put them on the side table. Then, when the flowers became an accepted event, she brought a low arrangement and put it in the middle of the meeting table. She thought someone might say "Get that off of there." But no one did. They seemed to like it. Some even said so.

When flowers on the table become an accepted norm, Alice baked cookies and bought fruit. She brought two plates to the meeting, putting them on either side of the flowers. People ate them, and said thanks. They started offering them to each other. As the weeks went on, flowers, cookies and fruit became the norm. Eventually one of the men asked, "Can you make pecan sandies? Those are really my favourite." Alice said, "No, but maybe you'd like to buy some and bring them next time." And he did. Others brought favourite things, and the group began to discuss who would bring what next time. A culture of gift-giving had begun.

Alice didn't need to bring food anymore, but she still offered flowers. Her colleagues began to ask her what kind they were, and sometimes even straightened one that drooped. Flowers and food became the first five minutes of every agenda, and the meetings ended with someone carrying the arrangement out to a place in the office where they could all see it through the day.

Over the many weeks of Alice's expanding intervention, the meetings lost some of their grimness. As people offered each other cookies, they began to offer each other the benefit of the doubt, so that they could start to listen. A little mutual regard began to surface, and people could bring some creative ideas forward without being squashed. Alice found that her own voice could now also be heard, and that her fresh perspective and gentle clarity were a welcome alternative to the habitual tone. Her colleagues began to turn to her and ask, "Alice, any thoughts on this one?"

Plenty of dysfunctionality persisted of course, but it was a start. When Alice told me her story it was still a work in progress. But she felt she had found a beneficial way to influence her colleagues, and that a more decent and productive workplace culture was starting to emerge.

Alice hadn't heard the rock tumbler metaphor when she did this. She didn't even really have a plan of what to do. She liked flowers. They helped her feel better at work. Finally she dared to see what would happen if she offered them to the group, not knowing whether she'd get shot down or not. Her design, if we can even call it that, evolved over time in small steps, the success of each step laying the ground for the next.

At the same time her intervention had all the hallmarks of a sophisticated container approach. The meetings were already intensely contained, inescapable. Alice didn't have to create that part. It might seem that there was plenty of friction there already too, but it was a destructive sort of friction. Rather than revealing people's brilliance, it was grinding them into sand. Alice offered another kind of friction: a cooperative generosity that could wear through the smallness and aggression that people were stuck in. Over time, this friction slowly wore out the armour people had put on and opened up the space for them to discover their own kindness, their trust and mutual respect. Or I should say, they could *re*-discover these qualities, which they had all along.

As with the oars taking charge at the Sea School, it wasn't really Alice who took charge here. Alice alone was powerless to change the culture of the meetings. She needed allies, and given her relationship with her colleagues and bosses, she wasn't going to find anyone on her team to help her.

From the container point of view there are many more allies available to us than just people. At the Sea School the oars were my allies. On the *Californian* tacking was an ally, and so was silence. I use the word "ally" because even though these things were inanimate, I could share with them the burden of having to turn a crew into an engaged and effective workforce. I didn't have to do it all myself. I had help from the oars.

In a situation where she could not at first rely on any colleagues for help, Alice found her allies in her flowers and baking. She realized that these ordinary things in her life might be details that could help in getting her colleagues unstuck. Since command is a matter of entrusting a duty to a worthy person, we could extend that idea to say that Alice's leadership consisted of entrusting to the worthy flowers the duty of shifting the team's behaviour. The flowers had tremendous if subtle power to soften and enrich. Alice let the flowers and cookies take command, and they provided, more effectively than she ever could, the conditions for the group to discover the qualities of mutual engagement that they had allowed to become submerged.

At this point we can go one step further. It's not entirely true to say that Alice did not take command. She couldn't at first, but her intervention created the conditions that allowed her to in the end. When one of the men asked for his favourite cookie she offered instead her first command, "Maybe you'd like to bring some next time." Why would I call this invitation a command? Because it was a way for Alice to start entrusting the mandate of cooperation and generosity to a newly worthy person. The man proved himself worthy of this trust by going out and buying cookies for the next meeting.

I talk about things as simple as buying cookies or arranging flowers in terms of "worthiness", "mandate" and "command" because one of the principles of container practice is that the simple, ordinary details of a situation can have as great an effect on shifting people's state of mind as any of our grand engagement strategies. In fact, when it comes to engagement, grand strategies often come a clear second to the details of the moment. The real power to influence our state of mind is in the ordinary things we're surrounded by every day.

Now Alice's command might have backfired, the man responding, "I don't bring cookies. That's your job, isn't it?" But things had already progressed to the point that such a response was no longer necessary. In this way, Alice took on the leadership of her department that the actual leaders were not able to take on. Though the actual leaders could have done the same. Faced with an intransigent and dysfunctional team, they could have created conditions that fostered cooperation and mutual appreciation, using changes in the environment (container) to create counter-stimulus (friction) that could wear out people's stuckness and open space for discovery.

As we think about how the rock tumbler approach might apply to our individual situations, it's helpful to keep two things in mind. The first is to take the indirect route. Alice couldn't hand out copies of an article on being a team player for everyone to read, and expect to get results. A frontal assault invites resistance. The goal may be to get from small to big and foster self-discovery, but the work is with container and friction, accepting that people's self-discovery is their own business.

The second point is that effective use of container and friction comes more from adopting the generous, trusting point of view than from learning specific techniques. Techniques are limited to what we can pull out of our bag of tricks. But each circumstance, each group of individuals is different, and we can't have a bag of tricks big enough for all of them. What worked for the teenagers at the Sea School wouldn't work for Alice's office team, and vice versa. If we approach the work of engagement with the attitude of "Let your people grow" and "It's not about me," and if we turn our curiosity toward the people we're working with, trying to understand and appreciate them, and if we look around us at the things that are already at hand to work with, that's all the bag of tricks we need.

It's hard to keep things dry on an open boat. On Sea School voyages, the food for the crew is kept in watertight plastic buckets. Since the Sea School's boat is completely open to the weather, and everything gets wet and stepped on, the buckets are the only way to protect the food and the gear.

Each bucket has all the food for a single meal, so the buckets are labeled "Dinner Day 1" or "Breakfast Day 5." Some instructors like to load the food buckets into the boat in order, so the first meal is forward at the bow, the second meal next to it and so on. That way it's easy to find the appropriate meal.

Other instructors let the crew load the buckets haphazardly, in no order at all. They don't do this because they're lazy or disorganized, but because without a system the crew has to have a greater awareness of where things are. When the cooks ask "Where's Day 4?" at dinner time, we go into search mode. Either someone knows because they were paying attention, or no one knows and we all have to look, reminding us that it helps to pay attention.

This is an inefficient way of finding the food but a very efficient way of developing an awareness of what's going on around us. Having a state of mind that is attuned to what's going on with the buckets is a step toward a state of mind that is attuned to what's going on with ourselves, our ship, our shipmates, our society. If we want to develop this kind of big view of what's going on around us, the buckets can help teach us how.

The point of this is not that we should scatter our inventory all over the warehouse so our employees can practice greater awareness of their surroundings. But it's helpful to notice how the way we interact with things that surround us day to day, like the buckets, can have an effect on our state of mind. For most of us, even though we may pride ourselves on our steadiness and mental toughness, in subtle ways our state of mind is often more fickle than we realize, easily influenced by the things we encounter. Working with the idea of container is very much about working with the way the world can affect our state of mind.

One way to understand container practice is to say that containers are made out of stuff. A ship at sea is pretty extraordinary stuff, and it's a shame we don't all have one. But that's okay, because none of us lack for stuff: rooms and windows, chairs and tables, lighting and decoration, clothes, toys, food, trees and gardens, roads and cars, on and on and on. Sometimes we may have special stuff: a child's birthday cake, a family heirloom, a sporting event. But even these special things usually involve some version of rooms and windows, chairs and tables, clothes and food and the rest of the ordinary details of life.

Our list also includes intangible stuff, like schedule, ceremony or hierarchy. Pretty much anything we might encounter in our lives is part of the container that holds our existence. We don't actually have to create containers. One way or another, we're always in one.

So let's come ashore for a while and look at how we can use the ordinary stuff of our daily lives to accomplish the extraordinary task of supporting people to discover the best in themselves, as Alice did.

If we walk into a room full of little gilt chairs with white cloth covers tied over their backs, or into a room of stacking plastic chairs, or a room with random cushions and bean bags spread around, we feel different in each room as soon as we walk in. The chairs alone have the ability to influence our state of mind.

On the one hand this is something many of us already understand intuitively. When one of our direct reports comes to our office to discuss a recent project failure we have the choice of sitting behind our desk and not offering them a chair, or coming out from behind the desk to sit together at the small table, or taking them across the street to a booth at the pub, depending on how we want the conversation to go. We know the power of chairs.

On the other hand, this is a power we are inclined to ignore. We think, "I don't have time for all this fuss. Let's just get this job done." But we miss an opportunity if we ignore the chairs.

One person who understood the importance of chairs, and the importance of container altogether, was Nelson Mandela, one of the best examples of generous leadership in our era. Many people now know about the rugby game as a nation building strategy depicted in the book *Playing the Enemy: Nelson Mandela and the Game That Made a Nation* and in the movie *Invictus*, but here's another more personal story.

Mandela needed to make peace with General Viljoen, an Afrikaner who led the militant white resistance to change in South Africa. After some negotiation, the general was willing to meet and talk. He expected this meeting to be between himself and his aides on one side of a conference table and Mandela and his aides on the other, with a lot of intense disagreement and animosity, possibly leading to some concessions on one side or another. Instead, Mandela invited the general to his own house. They sat next to each other in Mandela's living room, and Mandela himself served the general tea. Their few aides waited in another room. Mandela spoke in the general's native Afrikaans. By the end of the meeting the general had agreed to stop fighting. [1]

1. *Playing the Enemy: Nelson Mandela and the Game That Made a Nation* by John Carlin, Penguin Press, New York, 2008.

Of course it wasn't just the living room chairs. Mandela had an extraordinarily powerful personality and great skill with people. But he also recognized that in a difficult situation he could use all the allies he could get. Going straight to the conference table would have been the approach of "Let's get this job done." But the table itself would have been a further antagonist in the conversation. The comfy chairs, where they could sit together, were a disarming pacifier that allowed the general to feel, in his whole being, the possibility of peace.

It's interesting to note how the elements of container and friction merge in this case. The hospitable, gentle container of the living room also had a powerful inherent friction to wear down the adversarial attitude the general brought with him. The elements of container and friction are sometimes like this, not distinct elements to be collected and arranged, but naturally merged together into a single circumstance.

The living room, the tea, the conversation in Afrikaans, all these had to serve the container function of holding the general's attention long enough for their pacifying quality to work. The most disarming and pacifying room in the world would not have worked if the general had walked in and said, "I'm not meeting here. I'm not one of your neighbours over for an afternoon chat." In that case, the friction would have been too strong, the container too weak, and the moment of opportunity scuttled. But Mandela, the master of circumstance, knew what he was doing.

I call Mandela the master of circumstance because he was so amazingly good at creating circumstances with the power to support his countrymen to change their state of mind, to discover the best in themselves, to grow and prosper together.

He knew how to create circumstances with the power to accomplish his goals for him. In this sense he was also a master of container practice.

Most of us don't have that kind of natural mastery. Or perhaps I should say most of us haven't developed it.

Yet.

How do we know if the container we create in our own circumstances is the right one to hold the situation properly? Well, most of the time we don't know. Alice didn't know. She just tried something. At the beginning, or in unfamiliar situations, the practice of working with container is often a trial and error process. If the initial steps we take are modest, we can afford to experiment a bit.

I have found a few basic guidelines to be helpful in working with container, guidelines that can at least suggest an attitude to hold in trying my experiments. For me, these guidelines take the form of four questions:

1. "Is the situation contained, but not small?"
2. "What sort of boundary and protection do we need to offer, to prevent the wrong things from leaking in or the right things from leaking out? Are there 'gates' to influence how we enter and leave this protected situation?"
3. "Is the situation real?"
4. "Is the situation potent enough to do the work for us?"

Did Mandela know how to make the situation contained, but not small? Yes. The living room and house may have been physically small, but they brought into the meeting the elements of family and hearth, community and neighbourliness, peaceful domesticity, expanding the focus far beyond questions of power and the logistics of disarmament. Both men could see resolving their conflict in larger human terms.

Did Mandela know what sort of boundary and protection was needed? Yes. He welcomed the general at the front door and invited him into his living room, while letting the aides wait in another room. In doing this Mandela set a boundary that protected the simplicity and nonagression of the meeting; a boundary without leaks, that kept intimacy in and other voices out. He also let the way he welcomed the general and diverted the aides act as a gate, so the simple act of entering established the protected place.

Did Mandela know how to keep it real? Yes. His home was very real, and his hospitality was genuine, not affectation. The general did not feel manipulated, or as if he were participating in any kind of show.

Did Mandela know how to make the situation potent enough to do the work for him? Yes, the living room, the tea, the sincere hospitality, had a pacifying influence even before any protestations of peaceful intent that Mandela would have spoken.

What about Alice? Did she address these four questions as she began to design her intervention at the office? Not really. She didn't really feel as if she had a design or knew what she was doing, at least not at first. Still, she addressed these things intuitively.

Contained, not small—Alice recognized that she could take advantage of the fact that everyone was held together at the meetings already to do something to expand their perception and open up their state of mind. By doing something to cheer up the physical environment of the container, she could help people loosen their white-knuckle grip on their resentments and offer a bigger view of how they could be together.

Boundary and protection—She didn't at first have much control over the boundaries of the situation, or ways to protect her efforts. Anyone could have said, "Get those flowers out of here. This isn't a wedding." But she took the chance, and over time she created a new set of gates for the meetings: an entry point of appreciating and sharing her gifts before discussion started, and an ending ritual of someone carrying the flowers out into the office. It's not quite accurate to say she created these gates. Rather, she created the conditions that allowed these rituals to arise from within the group. This simple shift in how things began and ended helped to put a new sort of expectation around the meetings, which helped protect the more open and trusting attitude held in the meeting time between.

Real—She didn't try any hokey trust exercises or team spirit singalongs. She didn't say, "I brought us flowers because nature's beauty and fragility will uplift our spirits and open our hearts to each other." Her flowers and baking were ordinary things she did anyway. They were real and had the power of real things. She let these allies speak for themselves. In fact, introducing her flowers with a comment about nature's beauty would have blown a big hole in the container and all the power of the flowers would have leaked right out. You can't make a potent situation out of BS.

Potent—The fact that Alice's gifts could speak for themselves is proof that the situation she created was potent enough to accomplish her goals for her. The flowers and cookies were better at introducing gentleness to the meetings than anything Alice could have said. They held the attention and participation of her colleagues long enough for discovery to occur, which Alice could not have done on her own.

The Mandela and Alice scenarios offer two examples that show something about how we might approach working with container, but the idea of container is both broad and subtle. There are many ways to create a situation that holds our attention and participation, that engages us long enough for something to happen. Here are three more stories to consider, that illustrate some of the spectrum of possibilities. As you consider these situations, you can see how you think the four questions were addressed.

Bliss Browne, a very creative woman and wonderful story-teller, founded an organization called Imagine Chicago. It's a community development organization focused on tapping into the civic imagination of everyone, not just the "community leaders." Bliss tells this story. [2]

A young, pregnant, single girl in a distressed Chicago neighborhood wanted the boys in the project where she lived to stop shooting each other over drugs. She had no idea how to do this. Bliss asked her, "Do the boys want to be shooting each other? What do they really want to do?" The girl said, "They want to

2. Told by Bliss Browne at the inaugural lunch for Envision Halifax, Halifax, Nova Scotia, May 2004.

play basketball." There was a court in the project, never used and in disrepair. Bliss suggested the girl might try to get some games going.

The girl tore a page out of a notebook, wrote "Sign up to play basketball" across the top and put it up on the bulletin board in the entry to her building. In a few days the page was full. The girl panicked. Now what was she going to do? She had to get something going to meet all this interest. At a loss again, she went to Bliss, who suggested she ask the local merchants for help.

One store owner said he'd buy new basketball hoops and put them up on the broken backboards. Another merchant said he'd provide soft drinks for the players. Another offered snacks. Another offered a few basketballs. Some other men she spoke to offered to referee or just come to the court to back her up. When these things were in place, the girl posted the time for the first game, and the boys showed up. After some wrangling about how to form teams, they played. They played again another day. They kept playing. By the end of the year there were five teams from around the projects formed into a regular league. And then, because few of the boys had any kind of legal income, the girl and some of the other people involved got help from Imagine Chicago and created a job-training program for the league members. The job-training program filled up as quickly as that first page posted on the bulletin board for basketball.

If the girl, or Bliss, or anyone else, had gone into the projects to create a job-training program, the boys would not have come. Job training was not a compelling enough alternative to hanging out with their gangs. But basketball was. Basketball was the potent container that held the boys' attention and participation long enough to get them engaged in something other than their gang life. Any outdoor situation in as chaotic a place as an inner-city project is likely to be fairly leaky; there are so many disruptive forces all around. But basketball was a real thing in that community and it had its own power. Once the league got going, it had the strength to keep the right things in and the wrong things out, and was actually able to offer some protection against the seductions of the crime world. It expanded the boys' awareness of what was possible beyond the smallness of their gang territories, and it let them see in themselves the potential for being a useful, employed member of their community.

It isn't necessary to think of container as a big deal, like a basketball league. In fact it's often self-defeating to think in those terms. If you think of Alice in her team meetings, she would not have succeeded if she'd tried to introduce a big, new, complex team-building initiative. Her flowers were the right scale for the situation.

Sometimes, all it takes is a rock.

Prof. Eduard Franz Sekler, an old-world Austrian gentleman who is one of the patriarchs of the Harvard Graduate School of Design, had just such a rock. My first career was as an architect for eight years in Boston after finishing my master's degree at Harvard. For the last four years I ran my own practice. Professor Sekler was a major influence for me during the master's program, and when the chance was offered I jumped to take an architectural philosophy seminar that he taught. We met in a small room, six of us around a table. At the start of class he would set his papers and notes on the table and put his rock on top of them. We could tell by the way he placed it each day that he was very fond of his rock, though we didn't pay much attention to it.

One day the professor asked us to consider how design can influence the way we perceive the world. After some discussion, he picked up the rock and handed it around to us. We all held it, felt it, admired it. For the first time we really paid attention to it.

He then took the rock and stood it up on the table. It had always lain flat on his papers, but it had a flat end we hadn't noticed that let it stand upright. It shifted from mere rock to "object," and we admired it afresh. He moved the rock to a tall stand that had been sitting in the corner of the room all semester with nothing on it. Given this place of honour, the rock was now the most interesting thing in the room. Finally, there were track lights on the ceiling that we didn't generally turn on, but Professor Sekler flicked the switch and the rock was spotlit against the wall, casting multiple shadows and reflecting light from unexpected facets. It had become sculpture.

When the professor finally turned on the track lights we all burst out laughing with delight. We applauded the rock for its achievement, and we felt suddenly good about the world, optimistic and appreciative, eager to accept the rock's invitation to take a bigger view of the possibility in ordinary things. And Professor Sekler had not said a word. The rock did all the talking.

There's a sort of alchemy at work in successful containers, in potent situations. How can we transform things beyond their mere function, in a way that draws on their latent power to hold us long enough for us to see something new in ourselves? Professor Sekler's rock completely transformed, in a moment, the quality of our engagement with the room we had become familiar with all semester. It transformed the quality of our engagement with the philosophy of perception too. It was a one-shot deal, so the potency of the moment eventually leaked away.

But what if we had started every class from then on by having one of the students place the rock on the stand and turn on the track lights? And ended each class with turning the lights off and returning the rock to the professor's briefcase? We would have created a gate, a beginning and ending for the class that influenced our state of mind. Using design to influence how we see the world and ourselves in it was the underlying aspiration of all of us future architects. Using the rock as a reminder of this aspiration would have helped to protect our attention and commitment in the classroom. We'd have to be careful to keep it simple and real, not pious or precious, but ritual is also an important aspect of using ordinary day-to-day stuff to bring potency to a situation.

"Container" may not seem like quite the right word for the experience of Professor Sekler's rock, since it's just a single object. We might say that it shows a way of creating container from the centre, rather than from the surroundings. Or we could say that since container is about holding our attention and participation long enough for something to happen, and since it's about stuff, one bit of the right stuff can do it.

This simple approach of using a few choice things like a rock, rather than a complex array of things, is a helpful one to keep in mind. If we make too much effort, the situation won't seem real. Even in what is actually a complex situation, the best approach can be simplicity.

Let's say that you are responsible for planning a training program for a large and disparate group of people, and that you've rented a university facility for the purpose. What sort of alchemy can you practice with the complexity of the university building and all its components to create a potent ally for your purpose?

The ALIA Institute (Authentic Leadership in Action), where I serve on the faculty, is an example of this. ALIA holds annual weeklong, conference-style gatherings in Canada, the U.S. and Europe for a broad range of people who aspire to be agents of change in their various spheres and in society at large. We offer an unusual program, mixing corporate and organizational leadership development with mindfulness meditation and creative arts. The underlying intention is to discover the creativity and clarity that comes from letting go of our speed and preoccupation, to reveal our authentic, unburdened and highly effective selves. It's about leaving our claustrophobic state of mind behind and connecting with a big view.

The institute faculty range from CEOs and World Bank offi-cers, to international consultants, university professors, social innovators, meditation teachers, martial artists, musicians and calligraphers. The participants are equally varied.

We work hard to create a situation for each gathering that holds participants in an intensive learning experience, emphasizing the possibility of letting go of our speed and pre-occupation. This means creating an environment that helps us all to slow down and pay attention to our experience of the pres-ent moment.

Several times each day all the participants assemble in the main hall. This happens at the start and end of each day when mindfulness practice is taught. At other times we assemble for keynotes and plenary sessions on various topics relating to sys-temic change. One of the goals of the program is that people learn to bring the big view of their new mindfulness training, their ability to shed preoccupation and be fully present, with them into all the sessions and workshops of the week. How do we turn an ordinary, drab and featureless meeting hall into a container that supports this shift in our state of mind?

We have neither the time nor the budget to make over the room in any significant way. Rather than trying to do too much, we add a few elegant and vivid focal points, two or three versions of Professor Sekler's rock. We set up a low stage at the front, with a tall, narrow banner of the institute emblem on a white background. At the side of the stage is a large Japanese-style flower arrangement, a few feet wide and several feet high, spare and graceful. The other walls might also have a banner or other hanging, with an image rather than words. There are no catch phrases or exhortations displayed in the hall. No high-tech projections or stagecraft. Rather, the intention is to create a feeling of simplicity and elegance, the sort of richness and clarity that captures our attention but at the same time is very open-ended.

This way, during the sessions of mindfulness meditation, when the mindfulness instructor says something about the power of a simple, open-minded attention, the hall itself has said something about it already.

Similarly, we pay attention to gates, to the way we enter. Like most meeting spaces, the doors from the hallway outside open straight into the room without any vestibule, offering no physical transition to help us slow down as we enter. So we do two things. Outside the doors, far enough away to not create congestion, we place a table with a tablecloth and a flower arrangement. Behind the table is one of those ordinary blue curtains hanging from poles, found in every meeting facility, as a backdrop, with a decorative cloth or hanging on it. We put a small gong on the table, set in a stand. It makes a pleasing sound, and someone rings it to call people to the gatherings when it's time. People need to pass around the table and past the person ringing the gong, which slows everyone down as they move toward the doors.

On the inside, we use more of the blue curtains to create an actual vestibule, where people can park their coats and bags. For the mindfulness sessions, many people sit in chairs, but some like to sit on traditional meditation cushions, so they leave their shoes on racks in the vestibule.

By the time people have gone through these two spaces, they have had a chance to wind up their conversations and disencumber themselves of whatever they're carrying. They have slowed down, and are ready to enter the hall with a different pace, physically and mentally, than they came in with. When the mindfulness instructor says something about cutting our speed and bringing our attention to the present moment, the entrance itself has said something about it already.

Then at times the hall is rearranged with small tables and chairs, café style, for rotating small group discussions. Or a keynote speaker takes the stage, or the hall is cleared out for a session of movement improvisation. In each of these varied activities, the setup of the hall and the entrance continue to protect our intention to learn and engage with a slower, less preoccupied state of mind.

This attention to detail extends to the table settings in the dining room, which are handled by ALIA Institute staff rather than university facility staff. It extends to the way announcements are made, how the opening ceremony is conducted, and everything else about how the program happens. People come to the institute with a willingness to explore mindfulness meditation and creative process, as well as to attend workshops on leading change, so none of this feels false or out of place. And one of the main comments is always, "This program feels so different from an ordinary conference. How do you do that?" We do it by matching all the details at our disposal to the underlying purpose, with a unified intention. Every detail is a potential ally.

If we are magically transported to the office of high-end New York lawyers or accountants or hedge fund managers, we will know as soon as we open our eyes what kind of place we're in. Everything about it is designed to impress us with the power and position of the firm, and we stand up straighter and feel more rich and powerful ourselves. Visiting the Google campus with its "nap pods" and volleyball courts is a different story. It's not that we don't all work with container on a daily basis in various ways already. It's that we don't do it enough or as carefully as we could, so we limit our allies in each situation and more of the burden of engaging people falls on us.

Using our ordinary daily stuff to create potent situations can take limitless forms. It's not "Five easy steps to the perfect container." Sometimes it's creating a single compelling focus. Sometimes it's enveloping people in a powerful new environment. Sometimes it's tweaking the existing environment with a few appropriate details. Sometimes it's using what's already there in a new way.

The additional effort required to pay attention to the details of the situation may seem inefficient.

"These gang kids don't need games to play, they need jobs."

"I don't have time for your rock trick, just make your point."

"Let the facilities people take care of setup, we don't have time for that."

But urgency destroys capacity. Like the Sea School buckets, this inefficiency is tremendously efficient. The basketball, the rock, the vestibule, these are the kinds of things that deserve our attention, because if we relate to them properly they can form situations powerful enough to do much of our work for us.

Whatever approach we take, our goal is to form a container that has the power to hold us and protect us long enough for something to happen. A short-lived or leaky container, one we can easily get out of, doesn't cut it.

At the Sea School we offer professional development training for leaders and teachers called "The Container Principle: The Wisdom of No Escape." This is a particularly appropriate title for any five-day voyage in our 30-foot boats. There is no escape. Nothing leaks in. Nothing leaks out. Whatever comes up for people, we have to deal with it, which leads to a lot of self-discovery.

But containers are not prisons. Mandela says that he discovered the strength and wisdom to transform his country during his 27 years in prison, but in most cases holding people to our purpose against their will just makes their experience smaller and smaller. The best way to hold people is to engage them deeply enough that they hold themselves. Engaged people don't want to escape. They want to go deeper. A well-designed container offers the kind of invitation people have been longing for.

C aptain John Beebe-Center taught me how to work. John was captain of the schooner *Harvey Gammage* when I sailed aboard her as Chief Mate. It was my first job on a sailing ship, and I had a lot to learn, especially about work. The *Harvey Gammage*, a gaff-rigged schooner out of Boston, was known in those days as the "Heavy Damage." She was old and tired, and lots of things kept breaking. Captain John wanted any ship under his command to look sharp so the crew and I often worked into the evening, hanging over the side painting, chipping at rust on the deck fittings, coating the masts with linseed oil and tar. It was exhausting, tedious work, and I balked at the endlessness of it. I felt it wasn't really our problem. The ship's office should be paying to have the ship hauled out for a proper work period in a commercial shipyard, not leaving it to us underpaid and overworked crew.

Captain John thought I was a spoiled slacker. His view was that if the crew didn't take care of the ship, the ship couldn't take care of the crew, and in a storm that could be trouble. He was right. And my attitude was setting a bad example for the crew, which made him pretty angry.

Captain John rode me pretty hard much of the time, often reprimanding me for my work habits. He constantly tried to push me beyond what I thought were proper limits. We chafed against each other in a downward spiral of recrimination and resistance.

Then one evening at anchor, the electric generator that lived in a box on deck stopped running. Captain John didn't know much about engines, but he tried to fix it. I had the night off, and was getting ready to go ashore, where several of my shipmates had already gone. John had the generator taken apart on deck and as I passed he asked me to hold a flashlight for him for a moment. I grudgingly did, and asked if he knew how to repair engines. He said no, but he might figure it out, and if it ran we'd save a lot of time and money getting it fixed. If it didn't run, all he'd lose was an evening.

I couldn't believe it. Why would anyone waste their time like this? We should just get it fixed in the morning by a mechanic. It wasn't our problem; the ship's office should give us better gear.

As I held the flashlight I watched him work. He was covered with grease, a couple of knuckles were bleeding, the daylight was nearly gone, and he'd been crouched on his knees for an hour already. But he seemed content. He was gentler and more relaxed than I'd seen him before. Something about his doggedness, his private determination to do his best even if he failed, was suddenly compelling to me, and I saw him in a different light: not the unreasonable taskmaster, but the committed captain taking his responsibility seriously. I kept holding the flashlight.

We didn't talk. I knew nothing about mechanics and had no suggestions to make. He urged me several times to go ashore for my night off, but I stayed. It was a clear, quiet night, with a warm breeze and the sound of water lapping on the hull as

John worked. Eventually he had the generator reassembled, and it wouldn't run. He said, "Well, it was worth a try," and went to bed. I went to bed too, and my view of work had changed.

Container practice puts us in a place where some kind of friction can cut through the ways that we're stuck more effectively than anyone's efforts to unstick us. John's previous badgering had been the wrong kind of friction, and had only pushed me away. In contrast, his quiet doggedness was compelling. Something about the stillness of the night and John's undemanding effort combined to hold me, to create the container. The friction I needed was John's personal example, which, through the course of that long evening, wore through my sense of my own limits. Even then I would have resisted any admonitions from him about working harder, but he didn't try to turn the moment into a lesson. He just did his job, and let me see him.

As we say on sailing ships: "Friction is your friend. Chafe is the enemy." The literal sense of this is that when a sail is pulling on a line of rope in a strong wind 10 big men wouldn't be strong enough to hold on to it. But if we wrap that line a couple of times around a wooden belaying pin the friction of the line against the pin will do the work for us, and a single person can hold the end of the line and control the sail. So friction is your friend. At the same time, because the ship is constantly rolling and pitching on the seas, all the sails and rigging are constantly rubbing against each other, creating chafe that slowly wears everything out. If a line aloft chafes through and lets a sail break free or lets a piece of gear fall crashing to the deck, chafe can become fatal. So chafe is the enemy.

I take this sailor's phrase and apply it metaphorically to the rock tumbler image. You could say that the friction of the rock tumbler is also chafe in a way, since the point is for it to wear through the ways that we're stuck and so reveal our self-discovery. That's true. But too much friction, or the wrong kind of friction, can become destructive rather than revealing. Chafe rubs us raw and bleeding. The right friction wears away our obstacles and polishes our natural brilliance. The right friction gives the situation traction.

When we work to engage others, it helps if we constantly evaluate the flavour of the situation, and ask ourselves, "Is this friction or chafe?" Recognizing it is easier than knowing what to do about it, but recognizing is an essential first step. The more closely we pay attention to what's going on, the more we develop a sense of what's appropriate.

As with container, when we begin to work with friction, especially in unfamiliar situations, the practice is often a trial and error process. If the initial steps we take are modest, we can afford to experiment a bit.

But there are also some basic guidelines for working with friction that can at least guide our attitude in trying our experiments. These guidelines can take the form of three questions, with the basic underlying question being, "What needs to be added to the situation to help people get unstuck?"

1. "Is it real?"

2. "Is an edge of fierceness needed?"

3. "Is there an underlying kindness?"

The first question—"Is it real?"—we've looked at some already, and we'll touch on it again throughout the book. I don't think it needs a lot more elaboration, but I invite you to look for yourself at the stories in this chapter with this question in mind.

We'll start with the question of fierceness because it's powerful and also easy to misunderstand and misuse. It gets to the heart of using the word "friction" at all in the context of engagement. Neither friction nor fierceness sound very engaging, after all. If we're in a leadership position trying to engage our team, are we supposed to be fierce with them? What happened to "It's not about me?" What happened to generosity and trust?

The bottom line is still creating conditions that allow people to grow and prosper on their own terms. Our allegiance is to individual self-discovery. Our technique wherever possible is to take the indirect route and let the situation do the work. But sometimes a direct approach is needed. We want people to wake up to their potential. Sometimes they need a wake-up call, and we have to give it.

But here we enter dangerous ground. It is best to be cautious in thinking we know how to do this. The question "Is fierceness needed?" is a critical question, and most of the time the answer will be no. It is a means of last resort.

The Zen sword masters say, "If you have to draw your sword, you've already lost the battle." As we proceed in this chapter, let's keep this teaching in mind. If the situation has gone so far that what is stuck can be unstuck only by the fierceness of violent destruction, then we have made some blunder along the way. Anyone who thinks it's their job to hack away at the world with their sword in the hope of waking people up dulls their blade and creates a culture of fear and resistance. They turn friction into chafe, or worse.

In the following stories we'll explore different versions of fierceness, and we'll start with the most problematic, this question of taking it on ourselves to give someone else the wake-up call we think they need.

Nelson Mandela is again a good example to start with. Reconciliation between the races was the basis of everything he did during his presidency, so he did not employ fierceness much against his Afrikaner opponents. But he occasionally needed to practice fierceness to cut through the ways that his own people were stuck, understandably after years of oppression, in their impatience and vengefulness. He used his sword rarely. When he did it was freshly sharp and piercingly effective.

The old South African apartheid anthem, "Die Stem," was still loudly and proudly sung by the Afrikaners, but it was violently offensive to the nonwhite population, who had widely adopted the traditional African liberation song "Nkosi Sikelele" as the anthem of their newfound power. During the months before Mandela's election to president, as a new constitution and other policies of a fully democratic South Africa were being worked out in joint talks, Mandela's African National Congress party met to decide their position on a new national anthem.

Mandela was called out of the meeting to a phone call from a foreign head of state, and when he returned the party had unanimously voted to strike a blow against their old oppressors and ban "Die Stem," making "Nkosi Sikelele," which no white South African even understood the words to, the new official anthem.

Mandela said no. "You destroy the very—the only—basis that we are building upon: reconciliation." He told the party members that both anthems should be sung at all public events. He was immovable, implacable, and in short order he struck his party into submission and overturned their decision. They didn't even vote on it again. They simply accepted that he was right and that they—in what he showed them was their selfish need for retribution—had been wrong. Mandela's fierceness had brought his party back to full engagement with what really mattered: the reconciliation of the races. [1]

I don't know whether Nelson Mandela was saying to himself, "Is it sword time? Will my fierceness be properly calculated to cut and not undercut if I say this, if I say that?" I doubt it. I suspect that he came back into the meeting and was upset to hear the result, and spoke out spontaneously from his heart. Because he was not an angry man, not always on the attack as

---

[1]. *Playing the Enemy: Nelson Mandela and the Game That Made a Nation* by John Carlin, Penguin Press, New York, 2008.

some fierce and belligerent people are, his anger was likely to be an appropriate response to an inappropriate situation. Because he was not an angry man, his anger was trustworthy.

_____

I also am not an angry man, though I recognize that in my case this can be in part a fear of confrontation, a fear people like Mandela don't seem to be affected by. There is no comparison to be made between Mandela and me. That's not the point. But I know that losing my temper is one of the ways I'm able to summon my fierceness. This is true for many of us. We might think this approach would make our fierceness too random and reactive to be truly effective, but in fact I find that relying on my temper is quite trustworthy.

Richard joined the crew of the *Harvey Gammage* after my generator evening with John. Richard was brilliantly funny, with a dry twist that saw the delight and absurdity in every situation. He was always making us laugh at the world and at ourselves, though rarely at anyone's expense. He was charmingly self-deprecating, so in fact much of our laughter was at him. He was an invaluable protector of the crew's morale.

But Richard had even less of a work ethic than I had when I first came on board. He would rub his scraper slowly and gently against the flaking paint, admiring the view, remarking on what he saw or on random things that arose in his mind, and removing almost no paint. He would scrub the decks and leave large untouched areas, bone dry and obvious, and when they were pointed out to him he would have something to say about what their random shapes reminded him of. Captain John, of course, was always on his case, but because Richard was so thoroughly likable and cheerful he was hard to discipline. While his humour was a gift to us all, it did at times become an annoying smokescreen to cover his general uselessness. All of us at times wished he would just shut up and get to work.

Before long I saw another part of Richard. He seemed so modest and self-effacing, but he also had an underlying, contradictory arrogance. He thought of himself as the funny man; that was his role, and he expected to be accepted for it. Any further demands were unreasonable. To him, his humour, his general presence, were worth his berth and his paycheck. That's why my efforts to talk to him about his work didn't pay off. He'd agree and promise, but he didn't mean it.

Like most of the crew, I developed a real affection for Richard, and I was frustrated by his cheerful resistance to work. The rest of the crew felt that Richard's share of the burden of work kept falling on them. And I knew that if we didn't get the paint scraped, Captain John would be telling me about it, and I didn't have any of Richard's natural defenses. Since I was the Mate, it was my job to do something about all this. I didn't yet know how.

One day it was Richard's turn to clean the toilets (the heads as we sailors say). It was not a lovely job, but it wasn't awful. Richard kept putting it off, inventing pointless things he had to do, "helping" his crewmates with their jobs, distracting people with conversation. At other times I might have put a hand on his shoulder, looked him in the eye with a smile and said, "Richard, my dear, you do actually need to clean the heads." The warm and friendly approach matched his temperament and usually got him to at least start on the task.

But that day as I walked past him and reminded him, again, "Heads," he replied in his usual way, and it was one joke too many. I lost it. I stepped close and shouted in his face: "Richard! You're so full of shit! Clean the fucking heads!" Then I turned and left, not looking to see whether he moved or not.

My reaction stopped the whole crew dead in their tracks, and as I walked away they all looked at Richard. They looked with some sympathy, but also with the knowledge that I was right. There was part of Richard that was full of shit. In this new spotlight he went to clean the heads, did a good job, and didn't take too long.

When Richard finished the heads he came to me and said, "I did the heads. What's next?" What was next was a conversation we perhaps should have had much earlier, though I think it took my outbreak to create the space for it. It was my anger that got Richard to take me seriously. My anger had passed, so I could take him seriously. We talked about arrogance and entitlement. We talked about the gift and the trap of humour. I told him my John-and-the-generator story. Richard laughed that I had told him he was full of shit in the context of the heads, though I hadn't realized the connection when I said it. He talked some about himself, his own self-doubt, his narrow comfort zone. It was a good conversation. After that we had a code word. When he was slacking off I, or others in the crew, could say "Heads" and he would smarten up.

I very rarely lose my temper, swear or say anything harsh. As I said, I'm not one to seek confrontation, but I'm glad of that. I think it's this quality that makes my temper trustworthy. If I were the sort of person who shouted at people all the time, my interchange with Richard would not have worked so well. As it was, I had developed a relationship with Richard in which affection was the starting point and anger was exceptional. I surprised even myself. Since I rarely lose it, when I do it's generally for good cause, and I trust that. I did not trust the calculations I was working out for ways to cut through to Richard and wake him up. They all seemed false in some way and unlikely to succeed, which is why I hadn't really addressed the issue yet. When I lost it, it was as if the sword suddenly unsheathed itself without me. That's much cleaner. That is trustworthy.

The Aikido master Wendy Palmer is the founder of a program of training called Embodied Leadership. The program draws on her experience as a sixth level black belt but is designed for those of us who don't practice Aikido. Embodied Leadership is a novel approach to training that strengthens our personal performance under pressure in our work and personal lives.

In the training Wendy talks about two swords: the sword that takes life and the sword that gives life. The sword that takes life is sharp, sharp enough to cut something away. The sword that gives life is sharper, sharp enough to cut something into place. Fierceness can destroy what needs to be destroyed, that's not so hard to understand. The harder part is the possibility that fierceness could be creative. I can't say that I know exactly what this means, but I find the idea very provocative. The way that I take it is that sharpness could be so precise and accurate, and offered with such generosity, that it could place something new and needed in exactly the right spot.

I would not say that my anger cut into place anything for Richard. Imagining that we can go around cutting people into their enlightenment is the height of arrogance, and invariably ends up as chafe, or worse. What I would say is that my anger, which I can't claim credit for since it wasn't intentional, cut something into place for Richard and me together, perhaps for the rest of the crew as well. It was a wake-up call for all of us. The moment cut to the core of the issue about Richard: his humour was his strength and gift, and he also abused it. It protected him from looking at his shit.

The moment also cut to the core of the issue for the rest of us in the crew. How do we honour each other's virtues without enabling each other's shortcomings? If we had all been really good at that, the ship might have developed a culture powerful enough to bring Richard along to the point that he could engage both his humour and his work together. Good-humoured hard work. How great would that be?

It's one thing to have a group of perfect people who show up and work perfectly together. It's another to create conditions that support even difficult people to grow and prosper. The lesson that the moment with Richard taught me, that I have seen to be true in other situations since, is that we don't need to avoid anger at all costs. The raging tyrant is obviously not what we're talking about. Nor are we talking about being habitually irritable and out of sorts. But fierceness that is spontaneous and honest, without rancour or aggression, in a situation that can be followed up with cooler talk, can be friction and not chafe.

The Aikido sword masters aspire to protect their opponent as much as themselves. They do not train in hating and destroying their enemy, as Western militaries do. They train in equanimity, in how not to be an angry person, so they can cut clean.

Anger may be a fierceness we cannot premeditate, but there are other ways to be fierce that are more intentional. One is simple directness. Unaggressive honesty can be extremely sharp. I'll return to Mandela one more time to make this point, since I think he is one of the best examples of generous leadership I know.

When Mandela met with General Viljoen in his living room, the first bit of friction he used to cut through the general's initial resistance was his disarming hospitality and cordiality. The container he created was one in which it was essentially safe to be sharp. Then, in the course of the conversation, when the general said that he and his white followers had the power to stop the upcoming election by violence, Mandela replied, without raising his voice, that they could not possibly hope to win. The black and coloured population would never give up their new freedoms, they would resort to guerilla operations from the bush, and any white armed resistance would lead to decades of civil war. "Is that what you want, General, for your children and your grandchildren?" The general said no, and with that word, fighting was no longer an option. Mandela had not drawn his sword, but he had pulled it an inch out of its sheath, showing the blade. That was enough.

Mandela's was a respectful sort of fierceness, cutting perhaps, but not undercutting. If we remember to speak only to the best in the people we work with, even when their best is completely submerged by their worst, our fierceness can call out their best, and they can rise to the occasion. If we cut them off at the knees, they can't rise at all.

Speaking directly and honestly to the best in people also brings out the best in us. To see people's best, we have to look at them as directly and honestly as we can. We try to see them as whole people, not just the embodiment of our frustration. It takes more than fierce expression. It takes fierce perception.

This was certainly Mandela's gift. He saw things to appreciate in everyone, even his most vicious enemies. He actually managed to feel, and to show, genuine affection for Afrikaners whose families had brutalized his people for generations. François Piennar, captain of the South African Afrikaner rugby team, said of meeting Mandela, "It's more than just comfortable in his presence. You have a feeling when you are with him that you are safe." [2] Affection can cut away animosity and aggression. It can cut into place the deepest engagement of all: the engagement of the human heart. Affection too can be fierce.

I learned something of the way that affection can be an aspect of friction from Roland, who was the most difficult person I've ever sailed with. He was 15, an inner-city boy living in

2. *Playing the Enemy: Nelson Mandela and the Game That Made a Nation* by John Carlin, Penguin Press, New York, 2008.

foster care. We sailed on a seven-day Sea School voyage together, and trying to engage him and the rest of the crew together was a nearly impossible task.

For one thing, he wouldn't get up in the morning. As I mentioned before, in order for everyone to get dressed and going everyone has to get up off the oars that form our sleeping platform. If someone won't get up, we can't slide the oars back to the king plank in the middle of the boat and get at our gear. So when Roland wouldn't get up, everyone sat around shouting "Roland, get up!" and couldn't do anything else. I would command and condemn, which got us nowhere. Or I would kneel down by his head and talk to him softly, cajole or threaten or ask him if he really wanted to be such a jerk, if it was working for him. But he would either ignore me completely, or sit up for a moment cursing and thrashing to back me off, and lie down again. A couple of days we finally just slid him in his sleeping bag over onto a side bench to get him off the oars, and then worked around him.

Eventually he would get up, and be even more in the way. He'd refuse to do anything that needed to be done. If his task was controlling a sail while we were underway, he'd get tired and let go, allowing it to flog violently in the wind, endangering the people near it. His continual refrain was, "I don't care," and "It's not my fault." Even when he let go of the sail he'd say "It's not my fault." Once at supper he turned without looking and knocked a girl's hot tea out of her hand and said "It's not my fault." He was laughable, except for being so painful. The real problem was that he was right: he didn't care. Nothing I did could move him. He mistrusted my kindness, and my fierceness was no match for his.

He also would not make any effort to take care of his gear, despite my being on his case constantly about this. He was always losing his water bottle and his clothes in the bilge. The clothes would get wet with bilge water, and by the fourth day all his stuff was soaked. He was wearing shorts and his life jacket, the only dry things he had left, and he was freezing. I gave him two extra warm tops I had brought, and asked him why it was so difficult for him to take care of himself, and he said "It's not my fault."

There was another boy on the trip, Robert, who also hardly ever did anything useful, though at least he made an attempt if you asked him. He and Roland hit it off from the start. Their particular brand of social interaction was based on being incredibly coarse and offensive together. Everything was fuck this and fuck that, and they were given to outbursts like "Man, you got some big boobs, girl," or "Man, you are so stupid. Everybody see how stupid this guy is?" When we'd remonstrate with them, they'd reply, "Hey, man, I'm just saying..." or "I can't help it. It's true." It's nothing more than the rest of the crew were used to from people at school, there are often people like that at school, but living this close to it was hard.

We don't have a blanket no-swearing policy at the Sea School. We try to keep rules to a minimum. We work hard in recruitment to have every student crew represent a cross section of society, from the star of the hockey team and the valedictorian to the dropout to the kid on social assistance. The goal of the program is to help people learn to engage with good society by practicing in microcosm, so we need a complete society to practice with. However, rather than trying to impose our idea of good society with rules and "social contracts," our approach is to allow some deterioration of the social fabric so the issues become plain. In that way, people have more of a stake in resolving them. The trick is to allow deterioration that remains safe and to foster a resolution that is kind and instructive, not just a fight. We want friction, not chafe.

This can be quite hard to do, and Roland was one of the hardest challenges ever. Much of the time I felt near the end of my rope, and I was frequently on the verge of giving in and sending Roland home. He and Robert really did not seem to know how to turn off the foul language, the insults and the inappropriate comments. It was as if we were asking them to start speaking Hungarian. They genuinely seemed to think there was nothing wrong with their behaviour and were angry at everyone for giving them a hard time for just being themselves.

Interestingly, Robert had an underlying kindness that he just didn't have the right vocabulary for. At the end of the trip he went around the crew and said something appreciative about each person, even if it was "You are real fucking good with them stupid fucking knots." Even though he also almost never did anything useful, he was not obstructive, and the crew found ways to like him. But Roland was just steadily in the way and in your face, aggressive and demeaning, for seven days, with no escape for any of us.

Except when he wasn't. He would have unpredictable bursts of leadership and generosity. On a hot, calm day in the middle of the trip when we were drifting along under sail at a snail's pace and clearly were not going to make it to the island in the distance for hours yet, the girl in command suggested we take down the sails and start rowing. This was the right choice. We can row at two knots, so going slower than that is our cue that it's time to row. But we were hot and sweaty and no one was into it.

The commander didn't want to be bossy, so we drifted along. After a while Roland jumped up and said, "I'm rowing. Who's rowing with me?" No one replied. So he put out an oar and started rowing by himself, to pretty much zero effect on our forward progress, but with impressive enthusiasm. Shortly one of the other boys joined him, perhaps not wanting to be outdone by the misfit of the crew. The boat started to move just a little faster. Roland rowed fiercely and kept challenging the crew, without insults, to join him if they wanted to get to anchor in time for a swim before dark. Two others joined in, and eventually all eight oars were out, the sails were furled, and for over an hour the boat made consistently better than three knots, the fastest I have ever seen her go under oars. Roland kept the energy up to the point that none of the rowers ever asked for relief. It was impressive, and it would not have happened without him.

It's just that he had so little control over his moods. They controlled him. There were two versions of Roland, and spending time with him was like gambling. You never knew which version you'd get, though the odds were not in your favour.

So what to do? How could we engage Roland's good side rather than engaging the Jerk? Geoff, the assistant instructor, and I wondered a lot together what to do.

Much as we wanted to, we didn't send him home. We often felt like it, but we held to our trust in the power of the rock tumbler, and gave it time to work.

We couldn't simply wait, however. The whole trip was starting to turn into Rolandworld in the worst way, and we realized that we needed to address the chafe Roland was creating by taking care of some things ourselves. Standard Sea School practice is for instructors to be very hands-off, letting the crew learn from their own experiences and solve their own problems, even if that sometimes means learning the hard way and having real struggles with the problems. But the friction of having wet clothes wasn't cutting through to Roland's submerged self-reliance. The friction of being constantly criticized by the crew for being useless and in the way wasn't cutting through to his submerged initiative. So we began packing his gear for him and finding safe places for him to sit around uselessly where he'd be most out of the way. We couldn't do much about the offensiveness so we decided that when Roland and Robert got going we'd help the crew to not feed the fire, but just drop it. We tried to reduce the harm.

There's a Zen saying that if you want to control your cow, give it a big field. The tight fence that everyone usually tries to put around people like Roland is the high-voltage electrified kind, topped by razor wire and mounted with machine gun turrets. Everyone is always trying to cut him off at the knees. Geoff and I really didn't know what to do about Roland, but we realized we could try to emulate the wisdom of Aikido and protect our opponent as well as ourselves. By creating space for Roland the Jerk, without trying to fence him in with the hard time he's so used to, the Jerk got pacified, and the other Roland was able to surface now and then. We could see him sometimes trying so hard not to be the Jerk, and we got some brief bursts of helpfulness and good humour.

The technique that seemed to work best was being direct with him about his behaviour without trying to discipline him about it; offering a kind yet truthful mirror where he could safely see himself as we saw him.

On a morning when he was failing again to find his gear and get his duffle packed, and being offensive about it, I started, with great exaggeration, throwing my own gear around the boat and shouting, "Where the fuck are my fucking pants, you fucking fuckers. They fucking were fucking right fucking here and fuck, they're fucking gone." The rest of the crew were momentarily stunned, and then overcome with laughter. I'm the dignified, old man captain who rarely swears, so the effect was mind-stopping. Roland watched me sheepishly, grinning, and said, "Okay, okay," and continued to fail to get his gear packed, but quietly.

I also made a little rap out of "I don't care, it's not my fault, I don't care, it's not my fault," just those words repeated with a rhythm and a little dance, and the occasional "fuck" thrown in. Again Roland watched me, sheepishly grinning. I said to him, "Is that right? Have I got you nailed? Is that your theme song?" He said yes, and I asked him if he minded me teasing him. He said no, because it was true and he knew it.

This teasing was sharp and public. It was a kind of fierceness that could have been undercutting and demeaning to Roland. But it worked because in the midst of all this I also felt affection for him. He had a lovely smile, and was sometimes quite funny, in an offensive sort of way that I couldn't condone in this context, but if he were a New York standup comic, he might be rich. He was one of those people who wore his heart on his sleeve, in the sense that he wore his pain there, while keeping his heart far away from everyone, including himself. But his heart showed in the pain, and it seemed not truly malicious, but terribly sad. Being with him was frustrating and heartbreaking; I felt both anger and tenderness. Seeing these emotions in myself and letting them mix together was how I was able to relate to the confused and volatile mix of emotions in Roland.

The teasing allowed me to be playful with my anger and mix it with my tenderness. I could play with Roland as a way to say something he could actually hear. And the rest of the crew, seeing this, had some of their own resistance to Roland worn away too, so they could soften toward him as well. Roland was a mirror for all of us, and we began to discover in ourselves a kinder, happier way that we could engage him, which also seemed to help him engage the best in himself more often.

Friction spans a vast spectrum, from the fierceness of the sharpest sword to the gentle generosity of Alice's flowers. But these extremes, and all the points in between, are not as different as they might seem. Fierceness can be piercingly kind. Tenderness can be piercingly fierce.

The examples we've looked at so far in this chapter are exceptional cases. In the vast majority of situations, as my own experience has shown me in more failed attempts than successful ones over the years, we put ourselves on dangerous ground when we imagine we have the wisdom and the skill to wake other people up by our own actions.

As ever, the indirect route is usually the best. When we think about friction, we think first about the friction that the situation can provide, not what friction we ourselves can provide.

Another young trainee I sailed with had an amazing natural knack for making and fixing things, and for understanding how things worked. He also was a ball of energy, more likely to leap into things than to look before he leapt. His name was Ralph.

Ralph had been part of the building crew on the Sea School's second 30-foot expedition boat, the *Elizabeth Hall*. He sailed on the boat's 10-day maiden voyage from Halifax to Lunenburg as Leading Crew, the step between being a trainee and being an assistant instructor. So we gave him a lot of responsibility.

On the second to last day of the trip, when the whole crew had really come together as sailors and were taking command of the boat, we had a boisterous, rollicking sail in strong wind, rolling waves and bright sunshine. Everyone was thrilled, not just by the exciting weather but also by their new competence, handling the boat in these challenging conditions. We told Ralph to take command to bring us into the cove where we planned to anchor for the night.

The cove lay behind a rocky shore with only a narrow entrance into sheltered water. The wind was blowing strong straight onto the rocks and we were having a sleigh ride of a sail down the waves toward them. It had been such an exciting day that I had had to periodically remind Ralph and others in the crew to get out of their roller coaster mentality and pay closer attention to their work. It was the sort of day when delight can turn to disaster in short order. Ralph and I had been planning his approach to the cove, how to start early enough to have room to maneuver, when to take down which sails, who in the crew to assign which task. Then I watched to see what he would do.

Ralph was still pretty inexperienced. He hadn't often handled the boat in these conditions, and thought he could get the sails down easily as we did in milder conditions. He got stuck in his natural exuberance for the ride, and barreled along toward the coast much farther than I was comfortable with. Finally he gave the command to turn the boat toward the wind, get sails down and oars out for rowing. But when we turned back toward the wind and waves for this maneuver the roller coaster vanished immediately, replaced by the bucking bronco. With too much sail still up, we were being driven sideways toward the shore. Getting the sails down in that wind was a struggle, so we drifted farther. We finally got oars out and people rowing, but the wind was too strong to row against. We needed to turn the boat toward the entrance to the cove, but the crew was rowing with all their might, the person steering had the helm hard over, and still we were going backward, toward the rocks.

At this point I had to step in and take command from Ralph. He joined the rowers. When a boat goes backward, just as with a car, you have to steer the opposite way. If you want the bow of the boat, the front, to go right, you steer to the left. By having the person at the helm steer the opposite way, and getting the rowers to row on one side of the boat only, we were able to use our backward motion to get the boat turned. We were closer to the rocks than ever, but heading in the right direction, and now able to make progress. We rowed like hell for 10 minutes, everyone throwing their whole weight onto the oars, so much so that their butts lifted off the benches with each stroke, and we turned into the cove's narrow entrance and glided suddenly into still, sheltered water. I gave command back to Ralph, and he skillfully, if a bit shakily, got us safely anchored.

The crew were bug-eyed at what we had pulled off. Some of them, including Ralph, had been quite scared. The advantage of running a training program is that the instructors have so much more experience than the trainees that what is really a manageable situation for the instructor can seem like the brink of doom to the trainees. I let Ralph get closer to the shore than I was comfortable with, but not closer than I knew I could handle. We did not get so close to the rocks that we couldn't still stop the boat by anchoring and regain control at our leisure, and I had moved up next to the anchor in case.

Should I have taken control sooner and insisted that Ralph start to reduce sail at a more cautious distance? Was I wrong to frighten people so much? I don't think so. I would probably have been wrong to have done something *myself* to be frightening, to have added my own friction to the situation. But the boat and the wind could be frightening with impunity, because they were real. It was my job to be sure people were safe, but this does not mean I should have deprived Ralph of his panic. His panic can show him far more about his own caution and competence than I ever could. His panic can show him something about how he could polish his own natural brilliance.

What I needed to do was let his panic be friction, while being careful that it did not become chafe, grinding down his confidence and making him doubt his resilience. When we were safely anchored, we discussed the event with the whole crew, and I apologized for taking command from Ralph without asking him. He would certainly have said yes, but my abrupt rejection of his authority added needlessly to his sense of failure. I treated him like a kid. Instead, I should have let Ralph give me command, in front of everyone, like a junior colleague, rather than just taking it. At least I gave him back the command in front of everyone as we entered the cove so he could complete the day himself.

Often what seems to be the "friction" in a situation can itself be the problem; Alice's toxic meetings, General Viljoen's belligerence in Mandela's living room, Roland's antisocial moods. The friction that the container needs to hold is a different use of the word, something that can cut through or wear away the conflict or tension that's already there. Affection, kindness, humour, comfort, can all be very frictional in this sense, as we've seen.

Most of the stories I've told in this chapter have been about abruptly introducing an element of friction to the container through challenge or sharpness. There's also a slow, gentle aspect of friction that can be at least as effective, as we've seen in the case of sleeping on the oars on a Sea School voyage, or the inner-city basketball league in Chicago, or Alice's flowers, or tacking the ship in silence again and again. These stories were examples of trying over a period of time to shift the culture of the situation. We can think of friction not just in terms of abrupt and challenging intervention, but also in terms of slow and pervasive cultural intervention.

If the Sea School crew starts to freak out on a voyage it's because the abrupt, challenging elements of friction are working; wearing away or cutting through their complacency and comfort. But chafe is the enemy, so if the crew don't seem to be coping, the instructors have to step in. The point of stepping in is not to protect people from friction, however. Quite the opposite. We step in by offering a different kind of friction.

The additional friction is for the instructors to offer, in their own behaviour, a pervasive culture of kindness, gentleness, affection and good humour. A good-hearted culture wears away or cuts through the crew's attachment to irritation, blame and self-doubt. The rock tumbler approach creates a situation that is mirrorlike, and part of creating such a situation is ensuring that, whatever the challenges, people feel safe to look in the mirror.

We let all the friction be fully there, because that's what reveals people's natural brilliance. And we offer an underlying culture of kindness that helps people feel that, whatever they are experiencing, it's safe to proceed. The rock tumbler is full of grit, but it is lined with a cushion of rubber.

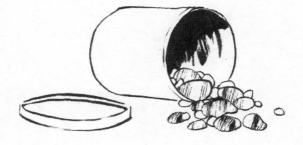

I have learned that expectation undermines trust.

Near the middle of a 10-day Sea School voyage, when the crew was starting to get good at handling the boat, two boys, Paul and Jay, were in command for the day. Since they were both veterans of other Sea School voyages, I expected big things from them.

Coming into a narrow, tricky harbour entrance I said, "You two are in charge, I won't say anything unless I have to." They conferred, and decided to make a cautious approach. They organized the crew to take down the sails and get six oars out so we could row in. We're much more maneuverable in tight quarters under oars than under sail.

But I thought, with the experience they had, that they should be up to sailing in, tricky as it might be, and I interrupted: "Wait a minute. You're not sailing in?" Paul and Jay were thrown off balance, their clarity shaken. I backed down and said, "No, I'm sorry, you do what you think best." But it was too late. They got us safely into the harbour, but their accomplishment was overshadowed by my question.

Who can know what might have happened if I had kept my mouth shut? They might have rowed in and had their own realization that they could have chosen the more challenging option of sailing in. This might have led them to reflect on what holds them back in their lives, why they hide from their own boldness. Or the confidence they got from rowing in safely, competently, responsibly, might have been the starting point they needed to feel that they could sail in next time someplace else. Or they might have already known they could sail in but realized that rowing was the right choice for them. Perhaps they were cautious by nature and felt good about that.

I stole from them all these possibilities with my expectation. The open-ended challenge of commanding under pressure might have provided a mirror in which they could see all kinds of things about themselves more clearly, but I directed them to see only one outcome, which they failed to meet.

It's not that I didn't trust Paul and Jay. I trusted them completely to handle the boat and the crew and get us safely into the harbour even under sail. In fact I may have trusted them to do this more than they trusted themselves. But this is a self-serving sort of trust, really more like expectation. I trusted them to do what I wanted, but I didn't trust them to do what they wanted. I didn't trust them to make their own discoveries.

Usually we experience mistrust as something that narrows our view of people, something that limits what we believe they can do. But the wrong kind of trust can be just as narrow a view, seeing only the outcome that we trust they will achieve. There is no room for surprise.

The kind of trust that supports people to grow and prosper on their own terms is the kind that does not anticipate the outcome. It's a trust based not on confidence, but on uncertainty.

We don't know what will happen, and we are willing to proceed on that basis.

Why would we take such an uncontrolled, scary approach to leadership? Aren't we responsible for good outcomes? Aren't we in a position of leadership because we know better than other people what should happen, and it's our job to tell them?

Maybe.

But probably not. That's a narrow, limiting view of what leadership is.

About halfway through another Sea School voyage I led, two of the boys in the crew, Brad and Nate, started blaming everyone else for not doing their share of the work, not pulling their weight. Until then the trip had been a complete love-fest, with everyone thrilled with the sailing, the coast, the new friends. But now people began to blow up at each other.

That evening we gathered for the regular crew "candle talk" that ends each day. We have a candle lantern made from an inverted pop bottle with the bottom cut off, which is our ship's light. We pass the candle lantern around the circle and when each person holds it they can talk about their experience of the day without interruption. The first few people were still mostly full of positivism as usual, trying to make nice, but when the candle got to Brad he started telling everyone that they were lazy, selfish, incompetent losers and that he was so sick of putting up with them and doing everything himself that he was going to swim ashore on his night watch and hitchhike home. He went on for some time in this vein, adamant about leaving, having swung from "best experience of my life" all the way to "this completely sucks and I'm out of here" in just a few hours. Nate sat with his knees up and his arms around them, head down on his kneecaps, and refused to say anything or look at anyone. When Brad's tirade was done, Nate just passed the candle to the next person without looking up.

The rest of the crew knew Brad and Nate were frustrated but really didn't get the extent of it until that point, and they were shocked. Everyone jumped to their usual habits of responding to conflict. Some became earnest friends, asserting that they hadn't known Brad and Nate were upset with them but that they were always approachable and hoped the two boys always felt they could talk to them, that they respected their feelings and so on. Others became guilty, confessing their shortcomings and promising to do better, but it had the familiar ring of a ploy to pacify their parents, and it didn't work on Brad. A couple of them said everything was fine, they didn't think they were shirking, Brad should just calm down and not get so uptight about things. The discussion went around the circle twice, with Brad repeating his attack a second time, now with more ammunition. We were all becoming dismayed.

Zoë was my assistant instructor for this voyage, and she and I genuinely didn't know what to do. Brad was getting angrier and Nate more withdrawn, and everyone else more confused. When the candle came to Zoë, she gave a balanced response to what people were saying, talked about the need for teamwork and learning and the fact that crews often encounter rough spots midway through a trip and that we would work it out. When the candle came to me, I could think of only two things to say. First,

I told Brad and Nate that I would really appreciate it if they didn't try to leave in the night because Zoë and I were legally responsible for them and would have to organize a search, call the police and all that. I hoped they wouldn't put us through that. Then, building on Zoë's response, I told everyone that I didn't have the magic trick that was going to resolve everything, but that I was glad they had got to this point because now they had a chance to go deeper and get real with each other, which in everyday life is a chance we often avoid. So I congratulated them and said I was happy for them, that they had arrived at this precious point of opportunity. What were they going to do with it?

The idea that I would congratulate them for their social collapse was strange enough to undermine the intensity and be a little reassuring, but the truth is we all went to bed angry or scared. Zoë and I lay whispering our hopes and fears together, but we didn't think we'd be up in the middle of the night chasing Brad. He was a basically decent guy and we thought my appeal would be enough. We were deep in the metaphorical fog, but perhaps morning would bring some clarity.

When we navigate in the real fog, we are repeatedly disoriented. We set a course and follow it by compass, but then we start to get nervous. The sound of a bell buoy that doesn't seem in the right place, a passing motorboat that we might expect to be in the channel but isn't, or a change in the direction the wind seems to be coming from, make us wonder if we've made some mistake, and we want to change course to adjust. But change by how much, in which direction?

Sometimes we just get struck by inexplicable doubt. We can't see 200 feet and the rug of certainty feels completely pulled out from under us. We're sure we're going in circles and that we need to do something. But what should we do?

The truth is that the sudden doubt is more disorienting than the fog. Changing course midway out of doubt is the surest way to end up on the rocks. To counteract this tendency, we cultivate the discipline of knowing what is trustworthy. We check the course we've laid on the chart, confirm how well the crew at the helm has been steering by the compass, determine that we are not in any immediate danger, and hold our course. Lacking something that we know how to fix, we don't try to fix anything.

The fog in Nova Scotia is thick and feels very solid, but it's fickle. It will lift for a moment now and then, giving us a glimpse of the shoreline, just enough to allay our doubt and refine our plan. Then it descends again, but our doubt doesn't descend on us with it. Thick as our doubt may feel, it's as fickle as the fog. Our doubt is not trustworthy.

If there's fog, we're vigilant and careful, and we trust the compass. The compass seems certain. If there's chaos in the crew, we're encouraging and warm, and we trust the power of the rock tumbler and the wisdom of our shipmates. We trust that the qualities of patience, empathy and mutual support are already present, if submerged, somewhere in the crew. We're not used to trusting things like this that seem uncertain, but over the years we have found these things to be trustworthy.

In this case the submerged ingredient was an older girl named Sarah. Getting to bed proceeded well enough that evening. Brad was still threatening but not so loud, and everyone else just wanted to get to sleep. Zoë and I could hear whispering, and since one of the whisperers was Sarah we didn't think Brad and Nate were plotting something. So we let them whisper. We couldn't hear what they were saying. My own fears were keeping me awake, but sometime after the first night watch change I fell asleep, while the whispering went on.

In the morning everyone was still there. The last night watch woke us up to a nice, warm day. There was obvious tension in the air, but no mutiny.

As people were dealing with their morning gear routine, Sarah came back to the cockpit to talk with Zoë and me. She told us that Nate had let his cigarettes get soaked, and he was out. That was a big part of his loss of heart. He didn't know how he'd get through the rest of the trip. Was there any way we could get ashore and buy him a pack?

This was something we could fix.

We don't have a no-smoking policy at the Sea School. These days smoking among the crew is rare. We regard smoking as a drug addiction and condemn it. However the last thing we want in a situation already designed to be stressful is somebody going cold turkey and freaking out, like Nate. Smokers are limited to three or four cigarettes a day, just enough to get their fix.

We needed to do what we could to make the trip manageable for Nate, for all our sakes. So we gathered the crew and told them what was up. We told them there was a public wharf a few miles away with a small store near it, and that breakfast needed to proceed quickly so we could get to that wharf and help Nate out.

This was all that was needed. Nate was very grateful and his spirits lifted immediately. Everyone still felt bad from the last candle talk and wanted to make amends with each other by working well together. We chose a commander for the day, one of the younger, more bumbling boys, figuring we should take advantage of the crew's team-mindedness to support him and let him show what he had in him. The commander coordinated an eager crew to start breakfast and get packed. While breakfast was being prepared we chose two navigators, pointed out the wharf on the chart and let them get to work figuring out how we would get there. We said to the crew, "You have the plan. You're on your own. Let us know when we get there." Zoë and I lounged in the sternsheets at the back of the boat, hugely relieved, while everyone got busy.

Busy they got. We were underway in record time. There were some nasty rocks off the entrance to the river, which the crew rowed around prudently. They then set off under sail across the bay for the wharf. It was a fine day with a good sailing breeze. The sails came down cleanly as we neared the wharf and the crew brought the boat alongside under oars, making an elegant landing. Everyone was very pleased with each other.

Zoë went ashore and got cigarettes for Nate and we all ran around and played games on the big public wharf. In twos and threes the crew went to the end of the wharf and talked. Zoë and I didn't know what they talked about.

When we all returned to the boat and cast off again, the troubles were resolved. The crew had found a new working arrangement for themselves. Zoë and I didn't know what everyone had said to each other, but we didn't need to. We could see the results.

Zoë and I couldn't have known whether our trust would pay off. The magic of the rock tumbler works, but sometimes it doesn't. Our experience over many years has shown us that if we write off a crew like this as something we have to fix, we'll be wrong. They discovered some wonderful friction for themselves. We trusted them to use it in their own way. They would never have had such a powerful experience of growth and renewed prosperity if we had told them what to do.

I tell this story of Brad and Nate not as an example of conflict resolution, but as an example of engagement. Many conflicts are far more complex and more harm can come from letting them run their course. But there is also creative energy in conflict, and people who are genuinely engaged with each other are more able to handle their conflicts in a mutually beneficial way. They can use conflict to build mutual trust.

Trust is really the only way to go if engagement is our goal. When we act without trust we impose our own idea. Imposing our own idea is not a favourable condition for engagement. It's a favourable condition for resistance.

———————

One of the most valuable things I've learned from being in positions of leadership at sea is how to proceed on the basis that I don't know. This approach has opened innumerable doors for me that a need for knowing would have kept closed. I have found this to be true of my work with teenagers at the Sea School, and equally true, with different methods, of my work with professionals.

Teenagers are trying desperately to understand the world around them, but they are not alone in being tormented by what they feel they don't know. We all know people of every age whose need for knowing has a desperate edge, which makes them cling like limpets to the "truth" of whatever they think they do know. Paradoxically, this need to know hampers their learning and limits their self-discovery. They want to proceed only on the basis of already knowing, which makes them difficult to engage in anything new and unknown. An encounter with someone who is confident enough to say "I don't know" becomes shocking and disarming. This is good. It creates an opportunity. Once the fortress of knowing is disarmed, we can enter.

To keep the defenses down I rarely give the Sea School crew a straight answer, so that after a while their dependence on me as the "leader" breaks down. They need to feel that in the big picture I am trustworthy, that they are safe with me, but they also need to learn to distrust me and trust themselves, with a trust that doesn't depend on knowing. Rather than knowing on my terms, it's better that they don't know on their own terms, so they are inspired to find their own answers.

The Sea School technique of never giving a straight answer may not be the best approach to take with employees, but the principles are the same. If I am in a position of leadership, those I lead need to feel that I am trustworthy, that we are heading in the right direction, but if trusting me undercuts people's trust in themselves, we have a problem.

One of my coaching clients asked me to work with her and her team in defining the vision for a new venture in the public health world. When we came to the point of defining the actual purpose of the venture itself, it got sticky. People wanted to think very broadly, about societal health in almost global terms, far beyond the scope of the actual work. This broad perspective was important because it was the source of inspiration, the reason they were so excited about the venture in the first place. But it was making the venture hard to define, and all the words on the flip charts were getting confusing. The team was bogging down.

There was time left in the session, and I let the bogging down thicken. We reached a frustrated silence and sat with it. People were looking to me for help. I could feel them thinking, "What are we paying you for?" But I didn't speak.

Then one of the people said: "There are too many words and ideas here. My mind is moving all over the place and I feel like I want to move the words around and see how they fit. Let's write each word on a separate piece of paper and spread them out on the table so we can move them around."

We did. Everyone got up, writing words and leaning over the table moving them around, putting them in groups, busting them up again and making other groups. Words like "welcome" and "demons" started to get put together (more on that later), and a big pile of discarded words grew on the floor.

The team realized that this wasn't a public statement of purpose, likely to be framed on the wall in the lobby. It was private. Just for them. It was their secret purpose, and in the end it didn't even include the more obvious words that might define the venture to the general public.

They had a debate about whether this was appropriate. It took some courage, but they decided to leave it as it was. They all suddenly felt completely clear about what they were doing, and fortified by their conviction.

This group thought I was there to lead them. But all I needed to do was create enough process to bring them to the sticking point and hold them to their awkward moment long enough, trusting that what they needed was already there. It just had to surface. The awkward moment provided the friction to wear through their stuckness and uncover their brilliance. My job was not to provide a solution to their stuckness. That was their job. My job was to help them find the friction of the awkward moment, and to create the container that would hold them to that friction long enough for it to work. And to trust that it *would* work. It usually does.

This approach may feel uncertain but it's actually quite trustworthy, because an awkward moment always emerges. Or a brilliant moment. Or a heartfelt moment. Because we humans are awkward, and brilliant, and heartfelt. We can trust in that. If we can create conditions that call out these qualities, that hold and protect them long enough for something to happen, we can support people to discover their own brilliant human gifts.

One of today's great practitioners of strategic leadership is Otto Scharmer, who teaches at MIT and works with multinational corporations and organizations to bring the full potential of their creativity and innovation to bear on their big systemic problems. In the book *Presence*, which he wrote with Peter Senge, Betty Sue Flowers and Joseph Jaworski, he tells this story. [1]

Otto was working with one of the world's largest international corporations, which had just completed a major merger with a competitor. A team of managers from all the key business units were charged with designing a process to develop new leadership skills that would allow these two merged competitors to compete effectively with the other businesses in their field, instead of continuing to compete internally with each other.

1. *Presence: Exploring Profound Change in People, Organizations and Society* by C. Otto Scharmer, Peter Senge, Betty Sue Flowers and Joseph Jaworski, Doubleday, 2004.

The project took four months. But on the last day the design for the leadership development process still wasn't complete. The Chief Learning Officer, who was head of the team, was supposed to present the design to the CEO the next day and secure the funding, and they had three hours left in the day. The creativity to synthesize out of all their work something innovative and powerful just didn't seem to be there, and it looked as if the project might end in failure. Everyone was getting very nervous.

Then Dave, one of the team members who didn't usually say much, stood up and with emotion in his voice said, "I'm really struggling here. I think I truly understand the pieces, but I just can't complete the whole picture." He turned to Otto and continued, "Can you help me? Can you explain this to me? If we can just see the whole, we'll have the breakthrough we need."

Otto didn't have an answer, and didn't respond. There was a painful silence, painful in part because no one in this group of senior professionals had ever publicly asked for help before. Dave's plea was a remarkable act of bravery. Finally, as Otto tells the story, it occurred to him to say that the missing ingredient for the group might be the willingness for everyone to speak and listen to each other with this same courageous openness.

Another person in the group agreed, saying "I think we could create any change we want to if we could just approach it with the kind of personal bravery that Dave just showed."

From that moment, everything that was needed to complete the design suddenly surfaced. Ideas and insights that had been held back now flowed, the four months of work came together as if by itself, and the team ended the day with a design for the Leadership Lab that they later implemented throughout the organization. This Leadership Lab was credited over the next two years with guiding two of the business units from "worst to first" in performance ratings. All because Otto didn't answer Dave's question.

———————

My friend Wendy Palmer, the Aikido master and Embodied Leadership teacher I referred to earlier, is fond of saying "You can lead a horse to water and you can drown it, but you can't make it drink."

A skill we can develop as leaders is the ability to refrain from drowning people by doing too much. As many of the stories I've told illustrate, doing nothing can be the most potent way to offer the generosity and trust that workforce engagement is based on. Often the most skillful thing is silence.

This kind of silence is not neglect. It's not withholding what is needed. It can in fact be the ultimate generosity, because it can convey complete open-ended trust, free from narrow expectation. It invites people to look to themselves and discover the best they have to offer. It invites the ultimate in engagement.

This kind of silence is composed of equal parts patience and attentiveness. Patience is needed to allow the rock tumbler to do its work, so we don't fuss with container or friction before they've had a chance to do their work. Attentiveness is needed to be sure we know what's really going on, that friction is not becoming chafe, that the potency is protected, that the situation remains appropriate. Attentive patience is fiercely alert. It demands that we apply a high level of intelligent effort and that we maintain our own deep engagement in the moment.

A simple aspect of refraining from doing too much is giving people space to be productive by not crowding them with micro-management, excessive workloads, endless meetings, pointless training and other unnecessary additions that make their experience claustrophobic. How many of us have wanted to tell a manager, "Just get out of my way and give me some room to do my work"?

One of the things to refrain from is filling up people's time with engagement strategies designed to engage them in the engagement strategies. This is why "engagement strategies" in general are suspect. They tend to be made-up, artificial additions to the situation, poorly synchronized with the real needs of the group. Let the engagement be about the work, and let the strategy be about getting out of the way.

But simply getting out of the way isn't enough. Giving people space to do their work is more than benign neglect. We offer space, not vacuum. Just as a host might clean up the house, prepare refreshments and invite guests in to enjoy themselves, introducing people but letting everyone have their own conversations, we can act as host and protector for people's work.

There is a large body of international work and practice under the umbrella of The Art of Hosting, a community of change leaders that I am part of that arose in Europe, Canada and the

US beginning in the 1990's. The central tenet is that innovative organizational change cannot be led, it has to be hosted.

The Art of Hosting community offers host training for "leaders, CEOs, managers, teachers—pioneers from all walks of life—who want to see and act wisely from a different perspective and practice of leadership, where other people's courage, creativity, intelligence and wisdom are set free." [2] The training, now offered around the world, emphasizes learning how to give what is needed and not give what is not needed, based on the practice of attentive patience.

Much of the work of the Art of Hosting is focused on helping people have conversations that really matter; conversations that are genuinely strategic, that include the points of view of all stakeholders, that lead to realistic action. The premise is twofold: one, that change imposed by a small group of "strategists" won't engage everyone else, leading to a lack of engagement that will be the main obstacle to implementing change; and two, that a small group of strategists will limit the possible outcomes compared with what could be accomplished by including the creativity and insight of everyone. The hosting role creates conditions that support genuine, complete interactions among everyone involved. A well-hosted situation holds a culture of "We did this ourselves."

We practice attentive patience not only in relation to the people we host, but also in relation to our own work of creating

2. Art of Hosting Home Page, www.artofhosting.org.

an effective container. It's not often possible to create a powerful container for people's self-discovery by suddenly making the perfect move. The best containers and the best friction are made by taking advantage of things that are already present in the situation, but those things may not yet be "ripe," or they may not all be available at the same time, or the people involved may not be ready to make a shift. We ourselves may need some time to understand the elements that are present and see how to use them.

It took twenty-seven years of attentive patience in jail, waiting for the necessary elements of international pressure, escalating violence and black organization in South Africa to accumulate and ripen around him, before Nelson Mandela could effectively act. However his long patience was not passive. He was constantly on the alert for new potential as circumstances slowly changed. He nurtured and guided the growth of all this potential, even from his jail cell. He did not try to force the situation prematurely, before all the elements that he needed were available to create the potent situation for national change.

This was equally true of Alice. She didn't know at first what elements of the situation she would be able to take advantage of. She just began with a small vase of flowers and let the potential of the situation reveal itself to her. Then she gathered and amplified that potential in incremental steps, with more flowers, with food, with an invitation to others to participate, slowly building the potent container and adding the appropriate friction. She trusted not only that the other people on her team already had what they needed to work well together. She also trusted that the situation itself already held the elements that were needed to create the potent situation. She was patient in discovering both.

We can trust in the self-discovery of the people we work with, and we can also trust in the self-discovery of the methods the situation makes available to us. The container, the friction, the potential of the situation—these too can discover themselves. With attentive patience, we allow them time to reveal themselves to us. The situation literally has a life of its own, and we can work with the circumstances of it patiently and on its own terms, rather than on ours, just as we do with people.

It can be tempting—especially in the risk-averse world of immediate benefits and guaranteed outcomes that so many of us often seem to be caught up in—to plan out every detail of our engagement strategy in advance so we feel that we know and can control exactly what will happen. This is naïve. We cannot predict and control people's experience. The attempt to control things at that level is actually limiting. We deny ourselves the freedom to take advantage of whatever arises.

The ancient Chinese classic *The Art of War* by the general Sun Tzu teaches about something called *shih* (the Chinese word is pronounced "shir" almost without a vowel). This is one of those words that really has no equivalent in English and is essentially impossible to translate, but it's very much related to the idea of attentive patience.

In the excellent recent translation by the Denma Translation Group, the translators have not tried to translate *shih*, feeling that any attempt to do so would limit its power. They let the text speak for itself and give us examples of how we might understand it in a few brilliant essays.

The text says:

The rush of water, to the point of tossing rocks about.
    This is *shih.*
The strike of a hawk, at the killing snap. This is the node.
Therefore, one skilled at battle–
His *shih* is steep.
His node is short.
Shih is like drawing the crossbow.
The node is like pulling the trigger.

And so one skilled at battle
Seeks it in *shih* and does not demand it of people. [3]

Why in the world, in a book on working with people on their own terms through trust and generosity, do I think it's appropriate to talk about war, battle and the "killing snap?" The last thing I want to do is give the impression that engaging people is like conquering them. No, no. Not at all.

But I find the idea of *shih* very useful because the container practice approach is all about making our *shih* steep. What does that mean? I interpret the idea of *shih* as "the potential of the situation." Every situation has potential. We engage our curiosity to discover this potential and make it "steep." As the commentary to the translation says, "The key to skillful action is in knowing those things that make up the environment and then arranging them so that their power becomes available."

3. *The Art of War*, Denma Translation Group, Shambhala, Boston, 2002.

We accumulate the elements and circumstances already present in the environment to create a potent situation, like water behind a dam. This potency has the power to create the rush of water, to toss the rocks about. This is a power far beyond what we ourselves could ever hope to muster. This is the meaning of "And so one skilled at battle/Seeks it in *shih* and does not demand it of people." Just as we cannot demand that people be engaged, we cannot demand of ourselves that we be omniscient and all-powerful leaders in designing and implementing our engagement strategy. Not only do most of us not have that kind of clarity and ability to inspire, it also creates a shallow, fragile kind of engagement that depends on us as leaders and invites a narrow kind of followership.

Rather than demanding that anything be present, we work with what is already present on its own terms. Discovering what we can use in the potential of the situation and discovering our own wisdom to use it go hand in hand. They are both "self-discovery." The skill of engagement is to let the real world be the real teacher.

*Chapter Seven |
It's All About Me*

I had a shipmate named Mike, who at a young age had been an engineer on the design team for one of the groundbreaking fuel-efficient engines at General Motors. He got fed up with the world of big business and took a job on the *Californian* as engineer on a voyage from San Francisco to Hawaii and back up to Seattle, which is where I first met him. He didn't know a lot then about sailing, but he never seemed to rest, and since the engineer on a sailing ship generally doesn't have that much to do in the engine room at sea Mike was often on deck or going aloft to help with sail handling. He learned fast. He learned navigation, and rigging, quickly becoming better at sail trim than I was. He became an excellent helmsman. When we suffered some hull damage against a wharf in a storm in Hilo he joined the crew replacing the planks. Whatever needed doing, he was always ready to dive into it, and he was always good at it.

Less than a year after leaving the *Californian*, Mike showed up again, as one of the Mates with me on the *Pride of Baltimore II*, sailing from Baltimore up the East Coast into the Great Lakes to Chicago and back. He was such a meteoric superstar that he was hired above me as Chief Mate, while I was Second. We had become good friends on the Pacific voyage, and our friendship deepened on *Pride*.

Mike could do everything aboard the ship. Whatever was happening, he took the lead, and he made it look easy. The captain would call him into the engine room when the engineer was having trouble. He figured out how to splice 12-strand samson braid line, which none of the rest of us could do. He took on the role of carpenter to design and build a modification to the deck boxes to store the gangway. He never seemed to take his off-watch rest time below in his cabin, but was always up working at something. And he was the guy that the one single girl in the crew fell in love with.

I learned a lot from Mike. His devotion to improving his skills, to being the best he could be every day, was impressive. You might say that he was the perfect example of someone growing and prospering on his own terms—the ultimate deeply engaged and highly performing colleague. It seemed that his "I can do anything" attitude showed what a very big view he took of things. His example was in many ways a model to the entire crew, and in this he seemed to be a natural leader. He was certainly the kind of person whose skills got him promoted quickly. He naturally gravitated to a position of leadership, and he took on this role with gusto.

But while Mike seemed to be so all-accomplishing he was fragile in certain ways. On an earlier voyage he had fallen in love with one of the women in the crew. She encouraged him, though the truth was she was pretty flirty with everyone. When it turned out that she was secretly sleeping with the Second Mate, Mike crumbled. He felt so unable to cope with the betrayal and manipulation that he left the ship under the pretext of a sudden family illness.

He was also fragile in other ways. On the *Pride of Baltimore II* there was a playful tradition of practical jokes, which caught all of us at one time or another. When we were washing down the decks in the morning we had to be careful not to let ourselves get cornered out on the chain plate channels or out on the bowsprit rigging, because whoever was running the fire hose might nail us with a stream of water. We would give each other booby-trapped birthday presents. I'm not a very large person and even though I was one of the officers I would sometimes get picked up and carried off by one of the crew or sat on ignominiously. In the tight quarters of a ship, having a way to let off steam together is a good thing.

When some of the deckhands played a joke on Mike his response was "You're going to regret that for the rest of this trip." This of course freaked out the deckhands, since he was their boss. It took me a while to talk Mike out of his offendedness, to get him to see that he could be flexible enough to hold the crew's respect without having to make them afraid of him.

In these situations and others like them Mike didn't seem to have the resilience to roll with the punches. He had a remarkable power to get things done on all fronts, to be sure, but I felt that he held on to his tireless activity as a way to protect himself from things he couldn't handle, using his role of being the all-accomplishing superstar, the person promoted fastest from newbie to Chief Mate, like a suit of armour. Armour is by nature small and claustrophobic, and in the big picture the superstar role turned out to be a narrow, limiting role: all about Mike, only about Mike. When Mike's armour got dented, by a betrayal or a joke, he got squeezed. Trying to protect himself with his role didn't work, for himself or for the rest of us.

There's a widespread belief that as leaders we need to fulfill the role of endlessly accomplishing great things, but we may be mistaking accomplishment for leadership. I don't believe they're the same. The all-accomplishing role may feel as if it springs from a big view of what can be accomplished, but it may simply be an overblown view, and the struggle to maintain the role can be exhausting. The paradox seems to be that a focus on great accomplishment can be small and limiting, and end up as a place to hide. The truly big view is unprotected.

The ways of engaging others we've talked about in this book involve personal qualities like generosity and trust and being able to hold a big view. These are qualities that many of us may feel we need to develop further in order to be as effective as we believe we could be. To use the techniques described in this book we need more than the techniques themselves. We need something of the temperament the techniques are based on.

One of the best examples of this temperament that I ever met was a boy named Peter on a Sea School voyage. He was barely 14 when he came on board, and he was young for his age. He was just as competent and quick to learn as Mike. He was quiet, easygoing and terribly homesick. He cried a lot from being so homesick, but never said he wanted to leave the trip. He never complained about anything, and often stepped up to help his shipmates with knots, navigation, setting the tarp up at night, all the things they wrestled with that he was immediately good at doing.

On the first night of the trip he was crying softly as we all sat together in the cockpit for candle talk. Not sobbing or sniffly, just a few tears on his face. He told everyone how homesick he was, but he said it was okay. The rest of the crew were very uncomfortable seeing another teenager's tears and tried all kinds of things to make him feel better. But Peter wasn't uncomfortable about his sadness and didn't encourage people's consolation. He sat up confidently, his emotion simply another presence in the circle, genuine and no big deal.

A few days later he was taking a turn as helmsman to steer the boat. It was a windy day and we were sailing for home with the wind strong and fair on the starboard quarter, which means it was nearly behind us. We roared along at our maximum speed down wave after wave after wave. The crew were exhilarated, faces laughing out from the orange and yellow hoods of their waterproof jackets, dripping now and then with the salt spray blowing over the boat. Peter had a hard job steering in those conditions. The strength of the wind kept trying to force the boat to turn, and the waves rolling under us would twist us right and left and back again. Peter had both hands on the tiller, which took some strength to manage, and he was braced against the side of the boat to keep steady, thrilled and focused. I sat next to him to coach him but he was such a quick learner that he was soon doing an excellent job on his own and I turned to look forward and enjoy the ride. I could tell by the way the boat continued to surf on the waves that he was doing just fine, and I began to talk with the rest of the crew.

After a while I turned back to check on Peter, and saw that he was crying again. Steering well, with his whole body and attention, with tears running down his cheeks. I asked him if he was homesick again and he smiled a big smile and said yes, very, he really missed his family. Then he turned forward again and continued to surf the boat down the waves.

The rest of the crew, fully caught up in their teenage worry about appearances, spent the first part of the voyage trying to fix Peter's problem for their own sakes, so they wouldn't have to see their own insecurity mirrored back to them by his tears. But Peter didn't need his problem fixed. For him it was a difficulty which he accepted without embarrassment, without turning it into a problem. He seemed to hold everything, even his sadness, with a light touch. He was not struggling to protect himself behind the role of being the tough teenage boy, or the role of being the awesome sailor, or even the role of being the homesick little kid. He wasn't struggling to protect himself in any role at all. Everything about him, even his homesickness, was simple, genuine and struggle-free.

Struggle can be exhausting, and tends to make us narrow-minded and self-protective. Not struggling to maintain a role, we can relax, and our state of mind can be big enough to accommodate whatever comes up. This was Peter's power. Being without struggle, he was inexhaustible. Whatever came up, he could handle it.

When the other teenagers finally understood this, they were awed by Peter. They'd never seen anyone like him. They'd never seen anyone who could be so genuinely sad and so genuinely engaged, so genuinely modest and so genuinely helpful, so genuinely relaxed and so genuinely accomplishing, all at the same time. Usually people in the crew struggle at some point with having to row or being cold and wet or not liking their shipmates, but on this trip Peter's example inspired everyone to see that they could be bigger than that. Whatever their troubles they could proceed with what they had, without turning it into a struggle.

Peter transformed that crew. He wasn't trying to take a leadership role, but his natural leadership helped his shipmates become one of the most resilient crews I've ever sailed with.

I don't know how Peter got to be this way. Maybe he had already spent years with the guidance of exceptional parents and teachers working hard to develop such an expansive view of his experience. Or perhaps he just had good genes. I can't say. There seem to be people who understand intuitively how to relax about themselves. But most of us don't. We have to learn it. I had to learn it. I'm still trying to learn it. It's a learning process that doesn't really end.

So actually it *is* all about me. It's about me learning to trust, me learning to be generous, me learning to step back, me learning to take the indirect route, me learning to cultivate the big state of mind. If I want to have any hope of becoming the kind of person who can genuinely think "It's not about me," I have to do some long, hard work on myself. It's very much about me.

What kind of work might that be? First it's the work of discovering a state of mind big enough to allow me to relax about myself, so that I'm not limited by the struggle to find protection in a role. Then it's the work of learning to notice how I am, in the moment, on the spot, throughout the day, so I'm aware of how I'm doing. (More on the second part in the last chapter.)

––––––––––––––

The Art of War talks about the "sage commander." In fact, the text is a primer on how to become and be a sage commander. In the contemporary commentary by the Denma Translation Group I referred to earlier, it says:

> The Sage Commander starts with himself. Thus his first question is not what to do, but how to be. Simply being oneself brings about a power that is often lost in the rush to be something else. [1]

Mike's meteoric rise felt to me like a rush to be a version of himself that didn't ring true. His focus on accomplishment seemed to be missing something. Some power was lost.

Peter on the other hand seemed to be genuinely relaxed about himself. The rest of the crew felt the power of this, and were inspired by it.

It wasn't Peter's accomplishments that made him stand out. It was his way of being. His simple unprotected presence helped everyone else in the crew shed the burden of their struggles too. Without even trying to be, Peter was one of the best leaders the Sea School ever had.

––––––––––––––

1. Essay on The Sage Commander in *The Art of War*, Denma Translation Group, Shambhala, Boston, 2002.

As leaders we may be tempted to assume the pose of leadership, or the pose of accomplishment, or even the pose of generosity. That makes it "all about me" in the wrong way. My accomplishment. My leadership. My generosity. To strike a pose we need a secure place to stand. But the world is shifty. When things go badly and the rug gets pulled out from under us, our pose becomes fragile.

Authenticity on the other hand is trustworthy. The words are nearly synonyms. If we are going to lead by trust, our most important attribute is authenticity. When we are caught in the rush to fulfill a role, we operate on the terms imposed by that role, and our point of view shrinks to the size of the role. When we are genuine, we can operate on our own terms and our point of view expands. Relaxing enough to be authentically ourselves is our defense against thinking "it's all about me."

This doesn't mean that the key to leading an engaged team is to let it all hang out, blurting out our fears and troubles. I'm not advocating the New Age encounter group approach. As leaders we often need to be circumspect, to hold back some of what we think or feel as a way of supporting others.

What it does mean is that leadership is more a matter of being than a matter of doing. The paradox is that by first paying attention to how we are, what we do can become unencumbered and all-accomplishing.

The *Harvey Gammage*, where Captain John got me to hold the flashlight while he worked on the generator, has come a long way since I sailed on her. She has new owners, she's well maintained, and is a respected part of the Tall Ship fleet. But before her more recent good fortune, she was known not only for being in tough shape but also (there may be a connection here) for being the ship where many in the profession got their start, as I did. You could say that the owner was generous enough to give aspiring sailors the benefit of the doubt by giving inexperienced crew a chance. Or you could say that he would do anything to cut costs, including manning his ship with incompetent wannabes who would work for a pittance. In those days, most sailors who had been around long enough to get established in their profession didn't go looking for work on the *Harvey Gammage*.

I was hired as Chief Mate because I already had a captain's license. Never mind that it was the lowest grade motorboat license you could get, limited to lakes and harbours, or that I had not yet used it professionally, or even set foot on a large sailing ship before. I had a license, which was probably more than any of the other applicants had, so I was Chief Mate.

But my ignorance was mortifying, and Captain John was appalled that I had been hired. It was his first command as captain, as I mentioned, which was in keeping with the owner's pattern of hiring only the inexperienced. But while he may have been inexperienced as captain, he'd sailed ships like this for years, been Chief Mate himself on many, and realized that in me he had no support whatever. He was not pleased.

The rest of the crew consisted of two college kids who didn't know up, an amateur naval historian who thought he knew everything, a revolving lineup of cooks aspiring to be sailors, none of whom lasted very long, and Mary Jane, age 54, who had retired early from her job to fulfill her dream of going to sea.

Thank goodness for Mary Jane. She had already been crewing on schooners for about three years. She was endlessly patient and generous in training the rest of the crew, including me, who was supposed to be her boss.

I had grown up sailing. I was a skilled navigator and had been working for a few years teaching sailing and coastal cruising and running small charter boats in San Francisco. But the *Harvey Gammage* was 130 feet long, carrying 5,000 square feet of sail. I was out of my league. I literally did not know the first thing about sailing a large traditional ship.

Mary Jane taught me that when I coiled the lines of rope and hung them on the belaying pins to stow them, the coils shouldn't hang down far enough to touch the deck. If they did, as the ship rolled and pitched the lines would rub back and forth against the deck and get chafe spots, weakening them.

Mary Jane taught me that when I climbed aloft in the rigging to handle the sails I should tie my knife to myself with a lanyard, so there was no chance that I could drop it and skewer someone on the deck below.

Mary Jane taught me not to call the captain "Skipper," a term that identified the user as a landlubber who watched Gilligan's Island.

In the myriad tasks and skills and protocols that a sailing ship demands, Mary Jane showed me how things should be done. Captain John tried to train me in these things as well, but at the start at least I resisted learning from him. I felt intimidated, pushed and browbeaten, and painfully aware that he didn't respect or trust me. This might have spurred me on to do my best, to show that I could meet his expectations, but instead it had the effect of spurring me to avoid contact with him as much as possible, especially if it might lead to any correction of my performance by him. Our relationship devolved into two intractable roles: the demanding, irascible Captain and the resentful, slacker Mate. You might not think that my role of resentful slacker provided me much protection, since it endlessly attracted John's anger. But it also allowed me to deflect that anger by saying to myself, "I'm not giving this guy the satisfaction of meeting his demands. He can't make *me* hop." I had made the situation about me in the worst way.

I don't defend my behaviour. I was not doing my job and was setting a bad example for the crew. As I said earlier, I had a lot to learn at that point about hard work, and in the end I learned a lot about it from John. But it was Mary Jane who taught me not only the skills of the schoonerman, but the delight of the job.

She too might have been expected to assume some kind of role to protect her rather vulnerable position of old lady trying to be an old salt in a crew of people nearly half her age. But she didn't seem to be burdened with much of that kind of baggage. She loved being a sailor on a traditional ship, and she was happy to share that love with the rest of us.

Engagement is a state of mind. One of the fruits of good leadership is an engaged and effective state of mind, a big view, in the people we lead. Mary Jane inspired something of this bigger state of mind in me, because she possessed it herself. She could teach me the hard skills of course, but John could too. It wasn't Mary Jane's seamanship that allowed her to engage me more effectively than John. It was her willingness to share her own joy in the work, and invite me in with her. She helped me relax about myself, loosen my grip on my struggle, and step out of my limiting self-protection into the big, glorious world of a ship at sea.

The fact that I continued to pursue a career on sailing ships I think I owe in good measure to Mary Jane. She helped me engage with the work on a personal level. I began to see that if I could acquire the skills of it and relax into the demands of it, I could also find the joy of it, and could make it my own.

A few years later, after I'd sailed as Mate on the *Californian*, *Anna Kristina* and other ships, I worked again with Captain John. We worked in Maine on a monthlong refit of two sail training and research ships, the *Westward* and the *Corwith Cramer*. Captain John's demeanor had changed a lot since our first job together. He was much more relaxed about himself, he knew how to draw on his strength of leading by example, and his own joy in the work was much closer to the surface. I had changed too. I had learned enough to be a decent Mate. Both John and I felt mature enough in our careers that we could be more ourselves. Without the struggle of self-protective pretense, we found we worked well together, and could become colleagues.

I continue to catch myself at times in what feels like a rush to be something else, and I see that in doing so I lose the power that is naturally mine. This points to what is for me the key to working with engagement: engaging my genuine self first so that I can genuinely engage others.

I see the truth of this idea reflected in the story of Alice. It wasn't some grand strategic scheme of hers that took control of those toxic weekly team meetings. It was her gentle, persistent generosity and her willingness to go out on a limb by bringing her flowers.

For Captain Andy and me, tacking the ship in silence, it wasn't our mastery of control or our exceptional execution that helped the crew to work so well together. It was the way we managed to set a contagious example of spacious confidence. Through the way we interacted with the crew we were able to model a way for them to interact with each other and with their work.

For Captain John on the *Harvey Gammage*, at first his way of being worked against him, and it was Mary Jane who was able to connect me with the joy of the work. When John allowed his quiet, undemanding doggedness to surface as he worked on the generator, it was that quality in him that finally allowed him to engage me too.

For Nelson Mandela, his new role as president was a huge role to fill, but he didn't seek to protect himself in it. On the contrary, he invited his adversary General Viljoen to his own living room, served him tea with his own hands and shared his concern for the fate of all their grandchildren. As much as any great deeds, it was Mandela's courageous sympathy and appreciation for his enemies and friends alike that defeated apartheid and unified the nation.

How do we avoid the rush to be something else and "be ourselves" instead? How do we even know what that is? Does "being myself" mean I have to be as creative and gentle as Alice, as courageous and sympathetic as Mandela, as quietly determined as Captain John, as modestly joyful as Mary Jane, as emotionally confident as Peter? What if I'm not like that? Wouldn't trying to become like that just be another way of rushing to be something else?

We can't all be Nelson Mandela, for goodness sake. But we all have some of Nelson Mandela in us already, and one of the points of this book is to say that "being myself" does in fact mean being like Mandela, like Alice, like Captain John, like Mary Jane, like Peter.

Obviously Alice, Mandela, John, Mary Jane and Peter are completely different from each other, and are each "themselves" in completely different ways. Yet they all possess qualities that allow them to accomplish many things and to achieve a high level of engagement in the people they work with. To be leaders of engagement, we can be ourselves and be like them too.

That's because we are like them already. We all possess the big state of mind already. It's our natural state. We all possess the inherent brilliance of generosity, trustworthiness, patience, bravery, wisdom, determination, and the list goes on. These qualities are more submerged in some of us, less submerged in others of us, but they are present in all of us. They are present in you. The selfishness, mistrust, impatience, self-protection, posing and so on that may at times submerge the best in you are just a cover-up, just brittle armour. They are not the "real you."

Whether you agree with me or not on the basics of human nature, I'm sure that you recognize in yourself times and situations where you find in yourself all the qualities you need to lead with generosity and trust, and that you are sometimes able to call these qualities up on the spot when you need them. And

I bet that when you call these qualities up it's not by summoning the great, perfect pose, but rather by relaxing enough to let your best come to the surface. We may be able to play the part of the masterful leader in control of everything, but generosity, trust and all the rest are not pretense. Rather than trying to summon qualities we think we ought to have, leadership for engagement works best when we let go of our resistance to being who we are. The power to engage others comes from being simply, decently, genuinely human, as we all can be, each in our own way.

How do we work with this idea on a practical level? Is there a technique for "being myself"?

We've been talking all along about techniques for supporting others. Now we apply these to ourselves. "Being myself" is allowing *my* generosity to emerge, *my* trust, *my* patience, whatever that looks like. "Being myself" is following the path of self-discovery on my own terms.

So we put ourselves in the rock tumbler. We look for potent containers that have the kind of friction we need to wear through the poses we're stuck in and reveal our submerged genuineness. We create the favourable conditions that support us to grow and prosper on our own terms.

The reason I left a successful architecture practice and pursued a career at sea, even after a difficult and rather discouraging beginning on the *Harvey Gammage*, was because I recognized that ships were the perfect teacher for me. I had loved boats and the water since childhood so professional sailing had always had a strong attraction for me. But I had also seen on many occasions how my experience on boats helped to cut through my small-minded self-protection and offer me a bigger view of what kind of person I might be. I could see that the intensity, the no-escape, the real situation demanding real commitment which comes from life at sea, could be a more powerful container for my own growth than my architectural practice ashore.

For similar reasons I went on to work with teenagers, an age much of the population will cross the street to avoid. Teenagers are brilliant at detecting poses, perhaps because they're trying on so many different ones themselves. They demand that I be real. I started the Nova Scotia Sea School because I recognized that teenagers, combined with boats, offered the right situations for me to grow and prosper on my own terms. They helped me discover that when I give up all the poses I learned from my family, my education and my early career development, I already have everything I need to be fully engaged myself and to lead others to engagement. This is true for all of us. We all already have everything we need. That's the promise of the rock tumbler.

How did I know what kinds of containers would be helpful for me? I followed my delight, and I followed my fear. Boats and teenagers delight me, and I also know how demanding they can be. Still to this day, at the start of every Sea School voyage I lead, I think, "Why am I doing this? What if there are lightning storms? What if one of the crew is impossible to deal with? What if there's an accident? I don't have to do this anymore, there are plenty of other instructors. I want to go home."

This always passes by the second day, but the demands of the voyage bring up my fears as architecture never did.

As my colleague Tim Merry, one of the stewards of The Art of Hosting mentioned earlier, is fond of saying, "If you're not at least a little scared, you're probably not learning very much."

———————————

Once in a San Francisco subway station I saw a small boy, about five or six years old, walking through the crowd holding his mother's hand. It seemed to me as if it might have been the boy's first time in the subway. The station was busy and loud, and the boy was small enough that he would occasionally get bumped by someone in the rush hour press of the crowd. His mother guided and protected him as best she could, but small as he was he was still too big for her to pick up and carry.

As he followed his mother he didn't cry or hold back, but he kept repeating in a small voice, "I'm scared. I'm scared. I'm scared." His mother said, "Yes sweetheart, I know." And they disappeared together into the crowd, the little boy holding his mother's hand and repeating, "I'm scared."

I thought, "Yes, sweetheart, I know too. I know just how you feel."

I thought that his mother was wonderfully wise. She held her son's fear with great tenderness, so he could learn to hold it himself. She neither stole away his fear, nor abandoned him to it. That is, she trusted her son's innate courage, and with her tenderness she created a safe and appreciative place for him to let fear in and walk with it. We can do this for ourselves too. We can make a container for ourselves that holds us to our fear with a sense of gentleness and self-appreciation. It's important that we not deprive ourselves of the chance to discover our fearlessness.

The story I told about my coaching client and her team trying to define the vision for a new venture in the public health world ended with the statement of purpose putting "welcome" and "demons" together. The group provided mobile health services to street people, many of whom were plagued by demons of all kinds. But it wasn't just those demons the group wanted to welcome. As they went further together in exploring their vision for their work, they realized that what scared them most, and what they most wanted to welcome, were their own demons; the emotional turmoil and self-doubt brought up by working in such an intense and challenging field.

These people had chosen to work in this field not only out of a desire to serve the public good, but also out of a recognition that learning to welcome their own demons and hold their own fears with kindness was what they wanted to learn for themselves. In the context of the rock tumbler, their work provided an intense and powerful container, but the friction they needed was the gentleness of self-appreciation, to wear out their self-doubt. With this intensity and this gentleness they found in their work the mirror in which to discover the best in themselves.

The street care workers are fortunate to have understood what they need to grow and prosper, and to have found the right container to help them. Or maybe I should say they are wise. Probably it's a combination of both. For many of us, our good fortune and our wisdom may not yet have come together in this way. We may feel we can't see how to put any of these ideas into action for ourselves, and we're stuck saying, "Okay, fine, but what do I DO?"

"The Sage Commander's first question is not what to do, but how to be."

The section on Practice and Application at the back of the book has more suggestions for what to do, but here's a simple place we might start. Jim Drescher taught me this.

Jim and his wife Margaret own the amazing forest woodlot at Windhorse Farm in Nova Scotia that I mentioned earlier. It's where the Sea School has harvested a lot of the wood we use to build our boats. Jim has studied sustainable forestry with many experienced foresters. One old-timer, trying to get Jim to relate to his work in the forest in a more discerning way, told him, "When you go into the forest, stop and state your intention before you enter. Say it aloud, in a loud voice."

Jim does this. I do it too when I'm visiting Windhorse Farm, and have taken to doing it at home too. It's strangely embarrassing to speak aloud even if I'm totally alone. No one can hear me, but I feel exposed. How weird is that? We don't like being exposed even to ourselves. But this can be a surprisingly powerful way of fulfilling Sun Tzu's command to start with ourselves.

I might say, "I come to the forest to go for a walk." Okay, but why? I might say, "I come to the forest to shed some of my burden and be refreshed by nature." Yes. Or does that sound a little hokey? I might say, "I come to the forest to show a group of teenagers where wood comes from." I might say, "I come to the forest to change the world by teaching the leaders of the future to care for the earth." I might say, "I come to the forest because I'm lonely. I come to explore this loneliness." I might say any number of things.

Sometimes when I hear what I say it sounds trite or incomplete or self-deceptive. Sometimes I even feel I need to turn and walk away without entering the forest, to collect my thoughts and try again. I really feel as if the forest rejects my lack of authenticity. Sometimes I realize that it's some role I've adopted that is speaking, and that I'm saying what I think my intention *should* be or what I think would sound good to others if they heard it. It can take a few tries to understand and accept my real motivation.

You might try this when leaving the house in the morning. Find a place where no one can hear you, perhaps at your front door, perhaps in your car, perhaps in the bathroom with the water running. Perhaps not in the shower; too comforting. State your intention aloud about some aspect of the day ahead.

Choose something that matters. Speak up, as if you are telling not just yourself, but the world you are about to enter. You can't do this silently in your head, you lose the power of it. Wait, and listen to it. Does it sound true? Ask yourself, "Why did I say that?" What does it tell you about yourself? How does it make you feel? If it doesn't feel true, try again. When you're satisfied with it, step forward into that intention. Carry it with you. Perhaps find a place at midday to repeat it to yourself, out loud. Speak up. See what sort of feedback the day gives you about it. See whether you understand your intention well.

Why do this? Because it's hard to be deeply engaged with life if we don't know why we even show up. And it's easier to be engaged with life if we feel we're showing up for the right reason.

———————

This is a micro-container practice. It has all the necessary elements.

You create the container for yourself by adopting the exercise as a practice, something you make sure to do regularly, every Monday perhaps, or even every day. You hold yourself to this practice, so it can hold you to your aspiration for new self-discovery. You do this long enough for something to happen; over a period of weeks, or years, or a lifetime. This container is inherently very leaky. All you have to do to escape is to say, "Nah, I'm not doing that. I don't like it." The discipline of keeping the container potent can be hard to keep up. But notice how you feel when you offer yourself that container, and how you feel when you deny yourself that container. When you deny yourself, is anything lost?

You create friction by speaking aloud. This is odd, embarrassing, uncomfortable. It can cut through ways that you're stuck by letting you hear yourself in a completely new and unexpected way.

This container and this friction create the conditions for discovery. Speaking to the world and listening to yourself is a mirrorlike practice. What you hear at first may be the speech that you've been giving all your life, or the platitudes your family taught you, or your fear. These are like looking in the mirror and seeing all the colours that people have been painting you all these years, or that you have been painting yourself. But we don't paint the rocks. The exercise of stating your intention is a kind of paint remover, and it gets you to look at how you are, your way of being, before you begin your doing.

On a Sea School voyage we sail between the endless horizon on one side, beautiful and sparsely inhabited bays and islands on the other, ocean below and sky above. Seals and dolphins come and go, gulls cry, a buoy blows its horn in the distance. We're on a 30-foot boat with 13 people, which gives us about 12 square feet per person, just enough room for everyone to have a place to lie down and sleep under the tarp at night. Being this crowded on the boat might be small and claustrophobic, but it's really up to us how big or small we allow it to be. Claustrophobia or vast space depends on which way we choose to look, in at our crowded boat or out at the big world.

In the early years of the Sea School, I sailed on a week's voyage with a group of girls from a Maine summer camp. None of them had signed up for a sailing adventure; it was just part of the camp program that year and they had to come. As one of the girls said to me after four days of sailing the coast, "I guess this is okay, but my idea of how you get around is, you call a taxi."

The girls found some protection for themselves from this unwelcome situation by playing Six Degrees of Kevin Bacon and other pop culture trivia games. Nonstop. For seven days.

No matter how magnificent the sunset, how still the morning, how thrilling the sail in a strong breeze under big white clouds scudding toward the horizon, they were oblivious. They preferred to have their heads down together competing for mastery of their small world of songs and movies and music videos, and they were unable to stop. It was all my co-instructor and I could do to get them to steer and handle the sails without them interrupting each other with a new pop-trivia challenge.

It seems to be natural that when we're stressed we tend to look in, to focus on ourselves and try to keep things small and protected, as the camp girls did. Perhaps it's because we all have so much stress in our lives, beginning at a young age, that small feels safe and eventually becomes habitual. We learn to carry our claustrophobic world with us everywhere.

Choosing to look out is harder, even with such powerful teachers as the sea and the sky. Big is scary. To be able to stop and connect with the bigger part of our experience, most of us seem to need help.

This is where we started this book, with the question of how to get from small to big. I believe this is a profoundly important question because, as I said at the beginning, engagement is a state of mind, and the source of deep engagement lies in being able to remember the big state of mind even when things feel smallest. When my view of the world expands, my engagement with it does too.

What's the answer to this question of how to get from small to big? Part of the answer is that it's not as hard as we might imagine, because we are already there. It's not that we have nothing but small and need to go find big. The big, spacious state of mind is our natural state. We have it already. All we need are conditions that support us to see it.

One of the indirect routes that we take at the Sea School for connecting with the big state of mind is the practice of what we call "outward turn."

Since claustrophobia or space depends on whether we choose to look in at our overcrowded boat or out at the big world, each morning—when all is ready but just before we raise the anchor and sail away from our night's anchorage—we space ourselves out along the edge of the boat and look out, in silence, away from each other toward the sea, the shore and the sky. Maybe just for five minutes, maybe for half an hour. We don't write in journals or read inspirational excerpts. We just sit quietly with the big world. We do this again at the end of the sailing day, once the anchor is down and before we dive into tarp setup and dinner prep.

In a situation like the boat, with so much potential for claustrophobia and self-protection, the practice of outward turn is a way we can give the crew the gift of space. When we turn out we expand our horizon, literally. The outer expanse awakens an inner expanse, and we find the space to wake up to the moment and to ourselves. It's a practice that helps us to make the moment mirrorlike.

This may seem like a curious way to approach a deeper engagement, by having everyone disengage from each other and all the tasks that the boat has waiting for us. It's a bit of a mystery, but it seems to be true: the most direct way to connect with the big quality of our experience is by simply stopping.

Outward turn is a stopping practice, and stopping practice turns our attention away from our preoccupation with tasks and doing, and opens up the space that's needed for a bigger state of mind, where we can discover something about how we are, at that moment, on the spot.

We also have to sail the boat on the next leg of the voyage, sometimes in strong winds or navigating in thick fog. We have to row, sometimes all day if it's calm. We have to get to a safe harbour, then set up the tarp between the masts, cook dinner, sometimes in the pouring rain. If there's a lightning storm in the middle of the night we have to evacuate the boat and go ashore. The next morning we get up, make breakfast, pack our gear and do it all over again. There isn't much time for sitting around on a Sea School voyage.

But even if there's bad weather coming and we have a long way to go and time is of the essence, we stop for outward turn. Why spend critical time on such seemingly unproductive activity? Because our state of mind is of the essence too. Whatever we do depends first on how we show up for the task: spacious and open, or preoccupied and narrow? So we start with how we show up. We start with how we are, in the moment, on the spot. To be able to notice how we are in the moment, we can take a moment to stop and look.

The goal of stopping practice is not to stop doing, but to bring to our doing the gift of space that helps us remember our bigger state of mind. Then whatever we do, we can bring our complete, unencumbered selves to the task.

We can achieve the panoramic state of mind, the sense of "spacious doing", even in the midst of very challenging tasks, where there's no chance to stop. The Sea School's oars are each 13 feet long, heavy and awkward. When we're fighting our way into a narrow harbour entrance against a strong current, or when we're in danger of drifting onto some rocks that could wreck us, rowing is all the engine we have. If people stop, the boat stops, and there's trouble.

But many of our trainees have never been in a boat before, let alone handled heavy traditional oars. How do you get a crew of inexperienced people to row together in sync, with power, for a long time, without the boat looking like a drunken spider?

You can try to set a rhythm by calling out, "Stroke! Stroke! Stroke!" But it isn't really enough to keep everyone's attention, and you just get hoarse and tired.

You can lead the rowers in a sea chantey to keep the rhythm. They don't usually know any chanteys, but you can teach them one, or they can sing "Row, Row, Row Your Boat," which everyone knows. This can help, but what often happens is that people get so engaged by the singing that they lose track of the rowing, and the drunken spider returns.

We've discovered over many years that the best way to synchronize the rowers is to say, "Okay, rowers, close your eyes, and listen for the sound of one splash as eight oars hit the water together." This feels like another mystery, but it's true. Rowers row better together with their eyes closed, in silence, listening to each other, than with any kind of rhythm-setting help.

Singing a chantey may feel energized and engaging, but it doesn't help the rowers row. The song adds an unnecessary layer of activity. When the rowers stop singing and row in silence listening to each other, they discover a sense of unencumbered, spacious doing, a sort of outward-turn-in-action, and they row well. Even in the midst of challenging activity, we can give the gift of space.

Being out in the big open world on the water has already brought an appreciation of spaciousness into the everyday experience of Sea School crews in a way that they generally don't find at home. Doing outward turn as a regular part of the start and end of each day in the boat helps the crew connect with this spacious experience and make it their own. An appreciation of spaciousness becomes more ordinary for them, so when we suggest they row in silence with their eyes closed, listening, it's not a great leap for them to bring their "outward turn minds" to the task. With this clear, unencumbered state of mind, they perform at their best.

Dr. Colin Guthrie is a past member of the Canadian Olympic sailing team and three-time national sailing champion. Colin's doctoral work led him to the growing field of "mental performance". He's now the mental performance coach for the Canadian Olympic and Paralympic sailing teams and other national teams. He's also taken his skills into the business world as a mental performance coach for senior executives.

Colin says, "The mind is the athlete." Physical performance training is of the essence for any athlete, but state-of-mind training is of the essence too. Colin works closely with his athletes to help them learn ways to keep their state of mind unencumbered by too much thinking, planning, worrying, second-guessing and all the other kinds of preoccupation that can consume them. Athletes will tell Colin that under the intense pressure of competition they lose because they psyched themselves out and let mental overactivity get in their way. They talk about getting all wound up and tight in their heads. They describe the experience of losing the big view.

Colin's job is to help them find ways to shift their attitude on the spot, in the heat of the moment, when they find they are stuck in this kind of self-limiting experience. Through the training programs he offers at the Canada Sports Centre Atlantic, Colin and I have been introducing stopping practice to his coaches and athletes.

Athletes can't stop in the middle of a race and do a little outward turn. By the time they re-engage with their more panoramic state of mind with a few deep breaths, they're breathing their competitors' dust.

But they can train to become more familiar with the panoramic state of mind every day, so that it becomes more ingrained in their basic attitude. You could say that when the Sea School crews do outward turn every day they are training their attitude, so when they need to row they can more easily shift their attitude in the moment, on the spot, to take advantage of a bigger state of mind. By including forms of stopping practice in their regular training regime, athletes can get better at shifting their attitude and connecting with the big picture in the middle of a race, on the spot.

Not all athletes are quick to accept that practicing being still is a useful technique for going for gold, but even in the go, go, go world of competitive sports, variations on the theme of stopping are becoming more prevalent. Colin and I have teamed up with Ed Hanczaryk, who's been rated one of the top golf coaches in Canada three years running. Apart from the extensive coaching in swing mechanics Ed gives his clients, he focuses as well on the mental performance side of their golf game. Colin, Ed and I have been developing ways of introducing stopping practice specifically for athletes.

The possibility of training in stillness is gaining acceptance in the sphere of sports at least partly because athletes have long had a fascination with the almost metaphysical experience of being "in the flow" or "in the zone." Bill Russell, five-time winner of the NBA Most Valuable Player Award and 12-time All-Star, led the Boston Celtics in the era when they were the most successful basketball team ever, winning 11 championships in 13 years. In his book, *Second Wind*, Russell describes "being in the white heat of competition, putting out the maximum effort, straining, coughing up parts of my lungs as we ran," yet holding a clear, still, panoramic state of mind. "The game would move so quickly that every fake, cut, and pass would be surprising, and yet nothing could surprise me. It was almost as if we were playing in slow motion." [1]

This experience is rare. Russell himself says it happened to him only a few times in his career. But the level of peak performance Russell describes is the holy grail of competition, when effort is effortless and the player seems to always know what to do. How can athletes achieve it?

1. *Second Wind: The Memoirs of an Opinionated Man* by Bill Russell, Random House, 1979.

Research on the "zone" experience indicates that it has more to do with the internal condition of the athlete than the external conditions of the game. The zone has been the subject of extensive research by sports scientists, and we are starting to know more and more about how athletes do achieve it. But the same level of attention has not been paid to how business and organizational leaders achieve their peak performance. Our lack of understanding of the subtle dimensions of peak performance in leadership, of the leader's internal condition, is what Otto Scharmer calls the "blind spot" of our time.

Why do our attempts to deal with the challenges of our time so often fail? Why are we stuck in so many quagmires today? The cause of our collective failure is that we are blind to the deeper dimension, the source dimension from which effective leadership and social action come into being. We know a great deal about what leaders do and how they do it. But we know very little about the inner place, the source from which they operate. [2]

Scharmer first came to understand the blind spot after conducting research at the MIT Sloan School of Management over a period of years in which he interviewed hundreds of leading scientists and entrepreneurs.

The men and women Scharmer interviewed were known for business and knowledge breakthroughs of all kinds. They spoke

2. "Addressing the Blind Spot of Our Time": An executive summary by C. Otto Scharmer, The Presencing Institute, www.presencing.com.

of their breakthrough moments coming from the experience of a relaxed and open state of mind that gave them unexpected access to a deeper intuition, a more panoramic understanding, than they were ordinarily capable of. Their experience of a stillness that gives birth to unexpected clarity is the deeper dimension, the source of effective action that we are normally blind to.

We're not totally blind to it. We all have "Aha!" moments and periods of flow in our work that come from - we're not quite sure where. For the group of innovators, even though they don't feel they really understand the "source" experience, what sets them apart is the extent to which they trust it and rely on it, and the extent to which they feel they can cultivate it. They recognize the importance of giving themselves the gift of space.

Scharmer described the experience of cultivating the deeper dimension that his subjects spoke of as "letting go and letting come." Letting go of habitual ways of thinking and doing, and letting come to us the bigger state of mind.

Stopping practice is a way of letting go. When we let go, the panoramic state of mind can come to us because it's already there. It's our natural state, just submerged by habit, speed and preoccupation.

That's why it's possible to shift our attitude in the moment, on the spot. We don't need time and effort to manufacture the panoramic state of mind. The small state of mind is the one we manufacture. We create it and reinforce it constantly with our habits, speed and preoccupation. If we can let that go, we'll find we already have what we need. The bigger experience is right there waiting, on the spot: the big world of an unencumbered state of mind and all-accomplishing action.

But we have to train in letting go and letting come.

This book is really about letting go and letting come. Letting go of control. Letting go of "leadership." Letting go of poses and the protection they offer. Letting go of "it's all about me." And letting self-discovery and expansive engagement come, on their own terms.

The letting go part is what we train in. The letting come part is what we trust in. It's trustworthy because what we want to have come is there already, just submerged.

How do we train in letting go and letting come? Not by pushing ourselves to try harder, to make that extra heroic effort, as we might train to accomplish other goals. We're not going to DO our way to a spacious attitude. Instead, we take the indirect route. Stopping, stillness, relaxation, genuineness, freedom from pose. They're all related. They're all aspects of the gift of space.

When we are well trained, when we become steeped in "outward-turn-mind," the unencumbered state comes nearer to the surface. It's not only already there, it's close. Then the indirect route can become very short. Short enough that we can shift our attitude on the spot, and over and over again bring ourselves back to an expansive and effective engagement with the moment at hand.

We don't need to make too big a deal of all this. All this talk of space may sound pretty philosophical, but it's also nuts and bolts. Bill Russell was playing basketball. The Sea School crews were rowing a boat. The innovators in Scharmer's study were inventing things and running businesses. It probably doesn't help to get all metaphysical about it.

Letting go and letting come is simply the practice of including space in our attention. Including "space" in our attention doesn't mean that we achieve some state of blissful nonthought. But when we practice a moment of stopping we can notice what we have been including in our attention, and choose what to include next. Training in letting go and letting come is training in choosing to include in our attention the spacious quality of our experience, for even a moment, over and over again, so that it starts to be included habitually.

As part of my own training I sometimes use one of those time minder apps on the cellphone to chime or vibrate every hour, and when it does, I stop for two minutes. I take some deep breaths, let the task of the moment subside, and see how I am, in the moment, on the spot.

Even if I'm in the middle of something, as often happens, I shift my posture, raise my gaze for a moment, extend my attention into the space around me and check my attitude. This moment of mini-space, as it were, is part of my daily training.

Momentary stopping doesn't have the drama of being in the heat of competition, or the communion with nature of sitting in silence along a wild and remote coastline. The power of stopping practice is not in the degree, but in the frequency. Even a little bit of spacious feeling, just a bit bigger than my normal experience, becomes powerful if I connect with it a lot. Developing a panoramic attitude is not like walking through a door. It's a life's work.

It's a life's work in the sense that we can spend our whole lives improving our ability to connect with spacious experience. It's also a life's work in the sense that it's about how we live our lives, ordinary moment by ordinary moment. Just as container practice can make use of the ordinary stuff we encounter every day, our attitude training can too. Can we make our daily experience mirrorlike?

In the shower, or the elevator, or waiting in line, these are all excellent places to practice stopping for a moment's "outward turn," since we're stopped anyway. Before we enter a meeting room, pick up the phone, or respond to an email, we can take a moment's pause, check our attitude and shed something of what might be preoccupying us. Making these stops a regular daily habit is a way of training ourselves to cultivate the panoramic state of mind.

Even in the midst of challenging activity we can keep checking to see if we're singing a chantey to ourselves, so to speak, and if it's getting in the way of our rowing.

There are more suggestions for how we can train our attitude through daily activities, beyond momentary stopping, in the Practice and Application section at the end of the book.

At the other end of the training spectrum from momentary stopping there are opportunities for more overt and intensive training in the panoramic attitude, if we're drawn to them. I've been practicing mindfulness meditation for 30 years, and it has transformed the way that I engage with my life and the work and people in it. I've done a few monthlong, even three-month retreats that have been powerful kickstarts to thinking bigger. Quests and retreats of various kinds can be excellent training.

But while retreat time gives my daily meditation more depth and strength, occasional retreats, like any kind of intensive training, are a flash in the pan. It's not the degree of stopping that matters most, it's the frequency. I try to make morning meditation as regular as brushing my teeth. If my time is very tight and I don't meditate, I at least pay attention to my hourly chime. Each hour of the day. Regular training is best.

The other aspect of our training is all the work we do to practice generous and trusting leadership, creating favourable conditions for others to grow. All the aspects of this book are ways to practice connecting with a bigger attitude. Giving the gift of space to others and giving it to ourselves go hand in hand and are mutually supportive.

If we can be generous enough to give what is needed and to refrain from giving what is not needed, then creating "outer spaciousness," so to speak, for the benefit of others, supports our connection with our own "inner spaciousness," and vice versa. That's the beauty of giving space. It benefits the giver as much as the receiver.

———————————

A sailing ship near shore is a nervous thing. We may think that being near land offers refuge if we need it, but harbour entrances can be narrow and treacherous, and the rest of the shore is made of rocks and reefs and sandbars all waiting to rip the hull out from under us. Keeping to the coast is false comfort, and keeps our horizon small.

What a ship needs is sea room, deep open water. The ocean may seem vast and unknown, but vastness has its own protection; the protection of being unimpeded and unbounded, free to see as far as the horizon, the mirrorlike horizon, where we see our whole world.

Horizon all around can be unsettling. We prefer knowing where we are. But then our experience becomes narrow, linear, and filled with nervous comforts.

We are not ships, and we cannot spend our lives on the other side of the horizon. But we can find our sea room, any time we stop to look for it, in any moment of the day. We can engage with the big world, completely. And we can help others to do so too.

Introduction

There are no "Five Easy Steps" to generous leadership and expansive engagement. I won't try to fool you with simplistic methods. Engagement is a state of mind, and making a sustainable shift in our state of mind as leaders, or in the state of mind of those we lead, calls for attentive patience—a subtle effort over time.

When it comes to time, most of us tend to feel deeply impoverished. We never have enough time. Undertaking anything that doesn't immediately appear to be the most efficient possible use of our time seems unproductive. But engagement that's more than a momentary excitement takes time. Training yourself in the attitudes of generous leadership also takes time. There's no way around it.

Can you afford to take the time? You can't afford not to. An engaged workforce is efficient and creative in its work, and allows you to be efficient and creative in your management. In the long run, creating an engaged workforce creates time.

Some of the practices and applications suggested in this section take only a moment, but need many repetitions. Some take bigger blocks of time but don't need to be done as often. You will get the best results by choosing some from each category, to give both breadth and depth to your practice.

Some methods in this section are specific practices or exercises with instructions for how to do them. More of them take the form of questions to help you examine your thinking and behaviour in a bigger context.

The methods offered here are a sampling of various approaches, and far from exhaustive. They will be useful as starting points, and are intended to spark your creativity in devising your own approach. Practice and application are a major element of my coaching and training work and I am available to support you if that would be helpful.

The methods are arranged to reflect the three main parts of the book:

Principles of Engagement

Techniques of Engagement

Engaging Ourselves

Part One—Principles of Engagement

Summary of the Main Themes

Generosity of learning

Arnold knew kayaks, and I didn't. Thank goodness he did.

We usually accept that teaching others can be a generous thing to do. Being willing to learn from others can also be generous.

What do your people know that you don't? Have you made an effort to find out? Have you created a culture in which people expect to learn from each other up and across the organizational chart as well as down?

It may feel a bit unsettling to encourage people under you to show that they know more than you do, but people are always going to know things you don't know. None of us are omniscient. An excellent way to engage people is to ask them to teach something, and then make the effort to actually learn it and make use of it.

Curiosity practice—If you are not naturally inclined to seek out what you can learn from your team members, you can start with safe territory. For instance, if your child is doing a history project, ask people when they're settling down to a meeting whether anyone knows about that historical period. Ask them a question your child is addressing, and let everyone hear the answer. Share the answer with your child, and report back what they say. Or if you've heard that one of your team members speaks another language, ask them to teach you some phrases. Actually learn the phrases, accept coaching on pronunciation, and greet that person with those phrases when you see them. The possibilities for learning are many. You can be as creative as you like.

The point is not to make conversation or single out people with little "relationship" tricks. The point is to train yourself in the habit of learning from your team. It helps to ask about things you have some genuine interest in, but you can also find ways of being genuinely interested in what each person can offer. You might be surprised at what you can learn, and from whom. Everyone has something to teach, though it may be submerged. You can create conditions for them to discover it and offer it. That's what makes this a practice of generosity.

Putting-to-use practice—The more immediately practical kind of learning is the kind that directly benefits the team's efforts. Do you have lunch and learn sessions where people can present or report to their colleagues on relevant topics in which they have particular expertise? If you do, set the example of asking questions, being careful not to sound as if you're testing them. Is there something in the tactical plan you're not clear on? Who can explain it? Let them explain it to you when others can hear too. In any situation, try to notice opportunities for people to show what they know in a useful way, and then help their teaching to emerge.

When someone is being a showoff or undermining the contribution of their colleagues, you can speak to them more directly about the culture of teaching and learning that you want to create. Or you might be able to find a way to let the situation do the work, by looking for things the showoff really needs to learn and for ways their colleagues can teach them, publicly, without humiliation. Ideally this would be about something truly useful to the person in question, that they can feel the immediate benefit of.

When some people are hesitant to offer what they know, you may need to more actively create opportunities for them and provide some protection for their first steps.

Then, when challenges arise and you're not sure of the best course of action, you will have trained your people, and yourself, to engage the full spectrum of your abilities, together.

Understanding "Their" Terms

Engagement is not the same as "buy-in." Buy-in implies people are buying what you're selling, and you have only one item for sale. It's not very engaging.

Engagement is also not the same as consensus. If people are deeply engaged with each other it may be easier for them to agree, but if you and I agree with each other all the time, one of us is unnecessary. Our disagreement can bring creative tension to what may nonetheless be a strongly engaged working relationship.

If you're spending a lot of time in your organization trying to achieve buy-in, or if your organization has a low tolerance for disagreement, those may be clues that you might learn more about "their" terms.

One practice for learning more about "their" terms is simply to ask:

- What do people feel is holding them back from their best work?
- Where do people feel their abilities are under-utilized?
- Do people feel good about their work (what they are able to do) but dissatisfied by their job (the parameters of their employment)? Or vice versa?
- What sort of contribution would people like to make to their workplace culture?

Specifically, for instance, do your performance reviews encourage people to clarify their aspirations? Not just their sales targets for the next six months or their goals for professional development in accordance with the "corporate values," but their aspirations for a full and rewarding life at work, or even beyond. This may not mean revealing intimate personal details, although it might. If someone aspires to care for an aging parent or overcome a fear of speaking to groups, is there a way that the workplace can support these aspirations?

Perhaps someone aspires to stop feeling as if they are one person in the office and another person at home. A commitment to expansive engagement means taking an interest in what the workplace can do to support even the most personal aspirations, if they should come up.

For more strictly work-related aspirations, what kinds of responses might people have to such open-ended statements as, "I would like to see my company be..." or "I would like to feel that I am...at work"?

The crew of the *Californian* (p.2) didn't aspire to be sail handlers or deck scrubbers or rigging repair personnel. They aspired to be Sailors, with a capital S; the kind of people who could tack the ship in silence or save the drifting launch. What are the equivalent aspirations in your organization?

Here's the essential question: How much can you expand the view you take of your people's "jobs," and how much can you support them to expand their own view too?

Employees First

An interesting case study of engagement strategies appears in *Employees First, Customers Second* by Vineet Nayar, CEO of HCL Technologies. The book presents a good exposition of a value that many organizations profess to hold. Southwest Airlines' past chairman and CEO, Herb Kelleher, for example, described his company's competitive advantage this way: "Our people. We take good care of them, they take good care of our customers, and our customers take good care of our shareholders."

Nayar at HCL seems to have been particularly successful at implementing this approach (average revenue per employee up from $37,000 to more than $50,000 a year, employee attrition down by almost 50%. A summary report by Forrester can be found at www.hcltech.com/insighthcl/forrester-hcl-efcs.asp).

He introduced a radical kind of autonomy for individual development teams, as well as a radical level of transparency, by turning the traditional organizational pyramid upside down. At HCL, shared services such as tech support and management are accountable to frontline development teams, not the other way around. They also put a premium on encouraging employee passion, creativity and innovation.

I question, though, whether HCL and the other places that promote "employees first" go far enough. Putting employees before customers or shareholders is good for engagement, but it's not quite the same as saying that people should grow and prosper on their own terms.

When you think of currently popular strategies such as putting employees first, ask yourself how far you're willing to go with that. If, for instance, a valuable employee believes they would be happier or feel more challenged doing another kind of job within your organization, or even with another company, could you truly put their personal growth first and support their move—even to the point of helping them with outplacement?

The question is, do you put people "first" but on your terms, so you can use their improved work to develop your *business*? Or can your primary objective actually be to develop your *people*, on their terms, using their work as the medium for their personal growth? The latter would be truly putting employees first. Can you see that such an approach is what will truly be best for your organization, and your society, in the long run?

This is a challenging question. Take time to explore it.

Command and Trust, not Command and Control

Giving command is not the same as giving directions. Your most prominent command can be the culture of trust you create.

Often the best commands are questions. If command is entrusting a mandate to a worthy person, your questions can help people discover new ways that they can be worthy of that trust. If someone comes to you with a problem, rather than solve it, can you use your experience to help them inquire more deeply into the problem so they can find their own solution?

Are you a consistent example of supporting people to step up and take initiative for things themselves, even if they may not be doing it exactly as you might do it? Do you command a culture of high standards without high control?

Are you a touchstone of personal trustworthiness in your organization? That is, are you a visible example of the culture of trust and trustworthiness you want to create? For instance, a CEO friend of mine made an important decision without consulting senior people who were out of town, and it upset them deeply when they found out. They thought she was undercutting their authority. The CEO called people together, with a facilitator, and went through a postmortem of the situation and all that led up to it. She was willing to accept her senior people's anger, listen to their point of view and explain herself without defensiveness. The result was not complete agreement, but everyone realized they could trust their CEO to be honest and straightforward and accept responsibility for her actions. More important, her example of willingness to have her trustworthiness examined, and the trust she herself displayed in her people to examine without rancour, was the most culturally powerful command she could have given.

This CEO had worked hard over the years to create the corporate culture. If you are at the stage of starting to shift in that direction, start small, and celebrate small achievements.

Generous Leadership

Pick an employee each day and take five minutes to consider what they need to flourish. What can you give them that would be a gift of generous leadership? This is different from what you could tell them, or how you could correct them. What task will they shine at? What person can you ask them to work with who will challenge them in a useful way? What problem can they address that will invite their creativity? What do they need to engage with their work more deeply on their own terms?

Part Two—Techniques of Engagement

Summary of the Main Themes

The Rock Tumbler: container, friction, discovery—p 39
    Contained, not small—p 58
    Gates: protection against leaking in and leaking out—p 58
    Keep it real, find allies in ordinary things around you—p 58
    Let the situation do the work—p 58

Friction is your friend, chafe is the enemy—p 75
    Friction is whatever wears through what is stuck—p 41
    Beware of thinking it's up to you to be friction—p 78
    The best friction is inherent, not imposed—p 94
    The sword that gives life—p 83
    Practice affection—p 86
    Underlying kindness—p 98

Don't paint the rocks—p 41
    Expectation undermines trust—p 101
    Practice attentive patience—p 115
    Give what is needed; don't give what is not needed—p 117
    Trust the power of not knowing—p 110
    Silence can be generous—p 115
    The leader as host—p 116
    The real world is the real teacher—p 121

The CEO and the chairs

Michael Scott was for many years CEO of Precision BioLogic, a medium-sized medical products company rated one of the Top Ten Best Places to Work in Canada. He's now Executive Chair.

For a few years now Michael has been pushing the chairs back against the boardroom table whenever he sees that they're out of place. He makes sure the chairs are evenly spaced and neat. He'll do this at the end of any meeting he's in, after people have left or as he's talking to someone who stayed behind. If he walks by the open door to the room and sees another group has left the chairs in disarray, he'll go in and arrange them, and whoever might be walking with him has to follow him in.

His employees began by thinking this was odd, not something worthy of the CEO's attention, or anyone's attention. Everyone's busy, why fuss with the chairs, what difference does it make? When asked why he does it, Michael says only, "I like it. It makes me feel better." He doesn't try to strategize it.

The chairs became a point of creative friction, rubbing against people's casualness, speed and preoccupation. Slowly the practice caught on. Now most meetings end with everyone pushing in their chairs as they leave.

Michael explains that the fact the orderly chairs make him feel better is not trivial. If he feels better when he enters the room, he feels better about the prospects for the meeting. He notices how the chairs affect his state of mind. The role of the chairs in helping to cut through casualness, speed and preoccupation has a subtly beneficial influence on the people who sit in them.

The point is not that orderliness is the best practice. Google thrives on unbridled creativity. If people start lining up the loungers and beanbag chairs in neat lines at Google that might be an indication that something is wrong.

Either way, try paying attention to the chairs.

The lunchroom

Michael Scott also says that for him a leading indicator of the health and productivity of his organization is the state of the lunchroom. If people take care in the lunchroom, they're more likely to be taking care in their work. If people aren't cleaning up after they eat, Michael becomes concerned about morale, quality control and customer service.

When Michael built a new building for the company he designed the lunchroom carefully—as a café (not a cafeteria). It's not grandiose, but it's not a windowless afterthought either. It is light and bright, with a view of trees and landscaping outside. People feel as if a comfortable, generous place has been made for them, so they're more likely to eat there than escape to a restaurant or eat at their desk. The lunch hour becomes a time when people get to know each other and exchange ideas across departments.

The room itself invites care. The materials are good quality. Michael spent money here, not on the executive office. If new people are messy, other employees set the example of taking care of *their* café.

When the New York City subway system was plagued with violent crime in the 1980's, the police didn't increase patrols to catch more of those criminals. The city focused on three things:

removing graffiti within twenty-four hours of its appearance, keeping the platforms clean, and catching people who jumped the turnstiles. Violent crime and robbery plummeted. Criminals realized the subway wasn't a free-for-all. This is a great example of the success of the indirect route.

Your lunchroom may not be like the NYC subway, but it's a place to practice the indirect route. If it's messy, can you do something other than tell people to clean it up? Would something as simple as a nice piece of cloth in the middle of the table with a decorative bowl of goodies on it affect people's attitude? What if you bought a new coffee maker? What if you yourself came in occasionally and washed some dishes?

Maybe your organization is big enough that you have a cafeteria rather than a lunchroom. How are people relating to it? Do they leave everything for the staff to clean up, or do they feel some responsibility to treat the space well themselves? What does this tell you about their state of mind, and what sort of indicator is this for the state of your business?

Starting practice—making a gate

We seem to be conditioned to find silence uncomfortable, as if something is missing, or as if we're being asked to solemnly "observe a moment of silence." But sharing silence together can be refreshing and calming, especially if people tend to rush into meetings from other tasks, towing their vapour trail of preoccupation with them.

Rather than dive into the content of a meeting as soon as everyone arrives, you can experiment with the friction of inviting the group to stop together for a moment to collect themselves. Take some deep breaths, maybe close your eyes, have a pause. Then proceed. To proceed well, start with stopping.

Working the room

This section explores the physical elements of container practice. The description is long because working with container focuses on the details of daily life, and there are endless details. You will be able to come up with many more questions to guide you simply by looking around you at the circumstances of your day.

Probably you are already careful with the environment and the hospitality you offer clients, colleagues and guests. What can you do to take this a step further? How can you make an ally of the simple act of welcoming and hosting, and induce in those present a big view of the possibilities of the meeting?

If you would like to experiment with this, you might keep in mind the questions I suggested in Chapters 4 and 5 as you approach a suitable meeting:

- Is the situation contained, but not small?
- What sort of boundary and protection do you need to offer, to prevent the wrong things from leaking in or the right things from leaking out? Are there "gates" to influence how you enter and leave this protected situation?
- Is the situation real?
- Is the situation potent enough to do the work for you?
- Does the situation offer a useful friction, that is not chafe?
- Is the situation infused with an underlying kindness?

Here are more questions.

Is the room the right room, or just the habitual room? Try walking into the room with fresh eyes. How does it make you feel? In your gut? Is that what you want everyone else to feel? Is there another room that feels better?

Is this, for example, a meeting that benefits from sitting around a table? Not just because people are used to a "boardroom" with a table where they'll have a place to put their paper, but because the separation and protection provided by the table is helpful. What if you met in comfortable chairs with side tables, like the photos we always see of meetings in the Oval Office in the White House? What if there were a counter-height table people could stand at and move around easily, clustering and re-clustering as needed? What if there were no table, just a circle of chairs?

To use the language of the rock tumbler, even the question of how best to accommodate people at a meeting is a version of friction, because the change of tables is intended to help the group cut through their usual habits of interaction to find a new and useful way of relating. Which of the options might best accommodate the group's need to wear through ways they might be stuck, and take a bigger view of their work?

You may not have much choice in these room details, but asking these questions helps you understand how the room you have is and is not your ally. At the least, taking time for this kind of inquiry is part of your training in understanding how ordinary things affect your state of mind, and the state of mind of the people you hope to engage. At best, you might see ways to make the room a better ally.

For the particular group of people and the particular purpose and the particular time of your meeting, would it help for the room to be more cheerful? If so, what can you do? Would it help for the room to be more formal? More rich? More ordinary?

If your office has the power trappings of a gleaming mahogany table does that mean it's the right environment for every situation? For your team, does the mahogany table foster a self-importance that isn't helpful at the moment? Would you be better off in a less formal space? For a particular client, do they chafe against the formality and elitism and need a different touch to relax enough to work easily with you? Do you need to come down off your high horse of being the one with the mahogany table so you can meet them where they are? Or is the gleaming table what is needed to inspire people to feel less impoverished about themselves?

Does a particular adversary need a different touch to let down their guard? Not so you can defeat them, but so you can more easily find common ground. What role do the water glasses play in this equation? Are they an offering of richness, or are they so fancy they're a distraction? What about the art work? And would you change any of these things because it might make people more comfortable, or because it might offer a useful friction to cut through some way that the situation is stuck?

The same questions apply if your room is drab, windowless, with concrete block walls. Would the people you're meeting with have a bigger view of the possibilities of the situation if the room felt more like a place they wanted to be? How much would that be worth to you?

Again, even if you don't have much choice in these things, the inquiry itself is valuable training. And you always have some choice. In the drab room, if you take a leaf from Alice's book (p.46), you might bring in a piece of cloth to run down the middle of the table, or a model racing car, or who knows what. For regular meetings you might bring a different thing each time. Children's toys. A photo off the internet. What might help that particular group engage with that particular purpose at that particular time?

A manufacturing company I know often puts one of their competitors' products on the table before people come in, so as soon as everyone enters, the room is already posing the question "What are we going to do about this?" Before the vice president leading the meeting says anything, people's creativity is sparked. Can you bring something that not only makes the space more engaging, but that actually says something about the purpose of the meeting that you then don't have to say?

You don't have to explain yourself to people when you do this. Just experiment. See what happens. Try again. See if anyone else starts to relate to the room more actively too.

The list of questions for you to consider goes on. The more you inquire into the ways your environment affects your state of mind and the state of mind of those you work with, the more opportunities for container practice you can discover.

Is there something you can do to the space to help it "hold" the participants. Should the door be open or closed? The drapes? Are refreshments in the room or in the hall outside? Is there distracting noise you can stop? When it's time for a break, should it be like a relief valve where everyone scatters, so you can gather them back with fresh energy, or is there another room to which everyone moves, with snacks and comfortable chairs, so the energy doesn't leak out? Which choice is better for this particular group and this particular purpose at this particular time?

How will people enter? What or who greets them? Who will sit where? Does where someone sits influence their participation in the meeting? What happens if you sit in an unaccustomed place?

The intention here is not to be cagey. The goal is engagement, not manipulation. The question you ask yourself is "What will help the people in this meeting expand their view of what's possible?"

It also doesn't have to be all up to you. You can ask your people the same question. "What can we do to this environment to help us feel more expansively engaged with our work?"

Attentive Patience—tell yourself to shut up

What happens when, in a situation where people might expect you to speak or where you habitually would speak, you don't? There can be an awkward silence you might feel the need to fill, but what if you don't? Who else might speak, and what might they say? If you speak, you'll never know.

What happens when you don't answer people's questions? Can you withhold *your* answer, and have the patience to let them discover *their* answer?

This is an indirect approach. Rather than telling people they should take a risk and offer new ideas, or telling them to figure things out themselves, or simply coaching them to put themselves forward and let themselves be heard, you can offer silence and see how they fill it. If the silence you offer can be attentive and patient, warm and curious, not cold and judgmental, it can be an effective and open-ended invitation.

If you undertake team-building activities, working together in silence can help people learn to pay attention to each other in a different and very revealing way. In some of the training sessions I do, I give everyone a piece of rope and teach them to tie a knot in silence. Then in silence we use those knots to tie ropes together for a useful purpose. There are also exercises of leading a group in silence through a series of maneuvers, and other training activities that use silent collaboration to shift the way people pay attention to each other. For more information on these and other training techniques, visit www.cranestookey. com/training.

Part Three—Engaging Ourselves

Summary of the Main Themes

Start with yourself—p 130

The first question is not what to do, but how to be—p 130

Accomplishment is not the same as leadership—p 126

Don't let yourself be protected by your pose—p 125

The big state of mind is our natural state—p 137

In your training, follow delight and follow fear—p 139

Spacious doing—p 151

Stopping practice—p 150

Outward turn: the gift of space—p 149

Our state of mind is of the essence—p 150

Let go and let come—p 156

Sea room—p 162

Email practice

(Adapted from instructions given in the *Search Inside Yourself* course in emotional intelligence and mindfulness, offered to employees at Google. With thanks to Chade Meng-Tan, www.chademeng.com; Mirabai Bush, www.contemplativemind.org; and Barry Boyce, www.mindful.org)

1. Compose email
2. Raise arms full length above your head and stretch them up
3. Lace fingers together
4. Bring hands down and rest behind your head
5. Lean back in your chair
6. Read email over
7. Edit as needed
8. Hit "send"

This is a momentary stop with an immediate practical benefit, checking that your email says what needs to be said and is okay to send. It could be nothing more than that. But following the instructions literally, particularly the upward full-length stretch of the arms before lowering the hands behind the head, makes it a body-stop as well as a mind-stop. It's hard to make the sort of stop that shifts our state of mind when the body remains tensely perched, nervously fidgeting or wearily slumped. In a momentary stop, let your body be your ally.

Peripheral vision practice

This is a practice that James Saveland, program manager for Human Factors and Risk Management at the Rocky Mountain Research Station in Fort Collins, Colorado (and an Aikido practitioner), has been teaching to smoke jumpers, the forest firefighters who rappel from helicopters in behind the fire. It helps them protect themselves from the kind of tunnel vision that an intense threat like a forest fire can cause. It's good training for anyone who wants to be able to adopt a more expansive view, literally and figuratively, on the spot.

Sit or stand still, looking straight ahead. Without moving your head, shift your attention to your peripheral vision. See what's in your peripheral vision as fully as you can, to the side, above and below. When your attention comes back to your frontal vision, shift back to peripheral. Do this for a minute, take a break, and repeat. This makes a good daily practice. It may seem literal, but over time it can shift how you choose to look at things attitudinally as well.

Outward Turn

The practice of outward turn (p.149) is something I've used when facilitating corporate groups, as a form of friction that can break the downward spiral when meetings get difficult or start to stall. Even if we only swivel our chairs around away from the table and look out at the walls of the room together, we still create an opportunity for our attitude to shift, on the spot. Changing our perspective and sitting alone while still feeling the presence of the group is a strong tool for cutting our momentum and allowing a moment of clear seeing to arise out of confusion. Even though we turn outward to the walls of a small room, we have turned outward from our even smaller stuckness and can re-engage with a more expansive attitude.

Dealing with Difficult People

What about the person who wants your job? In any organization there can be people for whom prospering on their own terms means that you no longer prosper at all.

This is difficult. I have no easy answer for dealing with people who feel most engaged when deep in toxic office politics. However my experience has been that the key is to introduce a sense of spaciousness into what is likely to be a claustrophobic relationship. Is there a way you can offer the gift of space?

Your first question is not what to do, but how to be. Can you be appreciative and disarming, drawing on the part of you that is like Nelson Mandela when he met with the white resistance leader General Viljoen who wanted him dead? (p.85) Can you be directly honest, and at the same time kind, in pointing out the true consequences of your rivalry, as Mandela did in pointing to the potential for decades of civil war? Can you understand what may be driving the other person, from their point of view? Can you feel affection for some aspect of their personality? In short, can your interaction with this person be based on your underlying aspiration to be kind, so the destructive chafe between you can shift into a useful friction, a strong, fearless gentleness on your part that might wear through their belligerence?

Probably you will need to shift your attitude in this way over and over again, moment by moment, as you continually fall back into your own resentment, defensiveness and fear. This is a chance to practice shifting your attitude on the spot, again and again, in challenging circumstances. It's an advanced practice. It's also a chance to practice the Aikido principle of protecting your attacker as well as yourself. Is there a way to channel Mandela, or Alice and her gifts, or Captain John when he stopped badgering me to work harder? (p.73)

If you feel that experimenting with this approach on the person in question might just complicate matters, you can develop your ability instead on other colleagues, people with whom you have a good relationship but have had a disagreement. Move yourself up the ladder of difficulty slowly, as your skill at shifting your attitude grows.

Embodied Leadership—Wendy Palmer

One of the best trainings in how to meet difficulty and pressure with an attitude of spacious generosity is the Embodied Leadership work of Aikido master Wendy Palmer. She works extensively with executives to help them bring a sense of "spacious doing" to their work and life, so they can engage deeply with the complexity of their situation while remaining clear and strong in their own integrity.

I have trained with Wendy myself, and can attest to the power of her approach. We can all be relaxed, generous, trusting and all the rest in relaxed, generous and trusting circumstances, but when suddenly the pressure's on, we revert to our habitual response. This response is not only emotional and psychological, it's also physical. Depending on our personal style, our body may hunker down, or press back, or collapse, sometimes in very subtle ways we're not even aware of.

Embodied Leadership offers training in how to recognize the subtlety of our physical response, and through physical exercises with partners as well as traditional Aikido sword practice, how to bring our inherent strength and clarity of purpose back into the equation, even under pressure. You can learn more at www.embodimentinternational.com/leadership-embodiment/ leadership-coaching.

"It's not about me" practice

The Tibetan meditation master Sakyong Mipham Rinpoche lives in Halifax, Nova Scotia, and has written a bestselling book, *Turning the Mind into an Ally*. I learned this practice from him.

Rinpoche is fond of saying, "If you want to be happy, think about others. If you want to be unhappy, think about yourself."

To explore this, you might try taking a moment each day to sit quietly without distractions and bring to mind someone you care about. Think about their situation, and wish them happiness, health and success. Think about what you might be able to do to support them. Try to make this vivid, not as if you're telling yourself a story about them, but as if they are actually there with you and you are extending your warmth and goodwill to them. Spend two or three minutes on this.

Then think of someone who is not close to you, someone you don't have a problem with but don't particularly care about either. Consider their situation in the same way, wishing them happiness, health and success. How could you help? Make it vivid.

Finally move to someone you do have a problem with, and repeat the exercise for them. This may be harder, but try to genuinely wish that they be truly happy and successful. Try to put yourself in their place, feeling what they might feel if they were happy and successful. Make it vivid. Is there any way you could help?

You may want to start with just the first part of this practice for a while. Then when the practice begins to make sense, try including the neutral person. When the practice feels strong, take on the difficult person.

It doesn't have to be people you would actually see that day, and it doesn't have to be the same people each time. The practice also doesn't have to lead to action. It's not about planning your interactions with those people that day. It's an attitude training, so it will probably lead to action if you hold yourself to the practice long enough. But don't beat yourself up if you see one of those people and don't enhance their happiness. Putting this practice into action can be hard. That's why you practice it in small doses, but often. Any shift in your behaviour from it, however small, is something you can be proud of.

Other "contemplative" approaches

If you are interested in more formal practices of mindfulness or contemplation as a way to train in letting go and letting come, there are many places you can turn. The good programs will avoid a sense of "don't worry, be happy" or "just do this simple thing and everything will be great" in favour of an emphasis on nonjudgmental self-awareness and expansive perception that grow over time based on your practice and motivation.

Here are a few references.

The Institute for Mindful Leadership, established by Janice Marturano. The Institute brings together mindfulness training and the actual, lived experience of senior business leaders. Their

motto is "Finding the space to lead." www.instituteformindful
leadership.org.

Washington Contemplative Lawyers, www.wacontemplative
law.blogspot.com.

The Law Program at the Center for Contemplative Mind in
Society, www.contemplativemind.org/programs/law. The center
offers other approaches to mindfulness as well.

Rapt: Attention and the Focused Life by Winifred Gallagher
(Penguin Press). How to let go of distraction and choose what
to attend to.

Wild Chickens and Petty Tyrants: 108 Metaphors for Mindfulness by Arnie Kozak (Wisdom Publications).

The Mindful Leader by Michael Carroll (Trumpeter). The
best leaders aren't those who take charge and make things happen. They're the ones who are willing to be fully human and
inspire the best in others.

Mindfulness in the Workplace, a starting guide to research
on the topic. www.mindfulnet.org/page9.htm.

ALIA Institute (Authentic Leadership in Action), programs
in mindful leadership and social change. www.aliainstitute.org.

Doorknob practice

A doorknob has a shape, a texture, a temperature, a quality
of movement, a sound as it operates. It has a feel in your hand.
It has a feel in your mind.

When you handle a doorknob, you can use that moment
as a small but complete container practice for yourself, with
container, friction and discovery. You can let the doorknob hold

your attention; you can let it hold the participation of all your senses for the moment you touch it. You can allow the various sensations you experience to act as friction that cuts through whatever preoccupation you may be stuck in. You can let this friction help you rediscover a sense of spacious doing as you turn the knob and enter the room. The whole process happens in a moment, on the spot.

These days doorknobs are not as plentiful as they used to be. If it's a crash bar or a metal push plate, the same approach can still work. Stop for a moment and connect with the physical sensations of opening the door and entering. Every time you do this, it can help you enter a more panoramic state of mind.

It's not just doorknobs you can do this with. Any physical sensation will do. In the middle of a meeting, lay your hand flat on a table. Feel the table and feel the muscles extending your fingers. If the air conditioning comes on, listen to the noise it makes for a moment. Really listen to it. You won't lose track of the conversation. You will make more room in your mind for listening.

In training yourself to shift your attitude on the spot, physical sensations are a powerful ally.

Walking down the hall practice

When you walk down the hall, or along the street, or through the parking garage, slow down. You will lose a few seconds getting to your destination, maybe even a minute. So what? Walk at a moderate pace, relax your shoulders, look up. You're doing a mobile outward turn. Throughout the day, you can bring a sense of spacious doing to simple things, even to getting your-self from one place to another. You can find your "sea room" anytime you choose to look for it, in any moment of the day.

To inquire about further coaching or training support for your practice and application, or to have me speak to your group, please contact me at crane@cranestookey.com.

A NOTE ON STORIES

The stories of my own experience that I tell in this book are all true. In some, names and circumstances have been changed to protect people's privacy. Stories from other sources that I retell are true to the best of my knowledge, and I accept them as true, relying on what I know of their authors.

THANKS

It's been my good fortune to be surrounded by teachers, without whom this book could never have happened. My father, who taught himself to sail with the tiller in one hand and a book in the other, and who taught his children to love boats and to value generosity. My brothers David and Jeffrey, who inspired me to think beyond the little bay I grew up on. And my mother, who never learned to sail, but who took care of everything else and taught me the meaning of "support."

Charles O. Aschmann, who taught me to love words. Prof. Eduard Franz Sekler, who taught me the importance of making a place. Bill and Kerstin Gilkerson, who showed me how to use boats and the sea to work with my state of mind. Captains Jan Miles, Bob Glover, John Beebe-Center, Deborah Hayes, Andy Reay-Ellers and Norman Baker, who showed me the techniques and the limits of command. Chögyam Trungpa Rinpoche and his students, who showed me myself and the bigness of the world. My wife Lesley, who teaches me what it means to be loyal and loving, uncompromising with creativity, and how to lighten up.

Richard Leckenby, Michelle Howell, Colin Guthrie, Zoë Nudell, Evan Cervelli, Denma Peisinger, Philippe Inacio-Goetsch, Dave MacCulloch, Katie Beck-Oliver, Phoebe Owen, Heather Kelday, and everyone else at the Nova Scotia Sea School, staff and students, who have taught me most of what I know about how to work with others.

For the creation of the book itself, my thanks to my insightful, kind and tough editor Barry Boyce, Liam and Margot Phillips

Lindsay for thoughtful copy editing, Jessica von Handorf for careful and elegant design, Susan Szpakowski and all the staff and faculty at the ALIA Institute for their encouragement and for expanding my horizons in so many ways.

And lastly, my teacher the sea, which has done so much to shape my temperament, my understanding of the world and of my place in it.

INDEX

ALIA INSTITUTE
Authentic Leadership in Action

ALIA is a convener of pioneering leaders and networks who are implementing positive change. It is also a place of applied learning and skill-building in the art, theory, and practice of authentic leadership and social innovation.

ALIA recognizes that leadership is concentrated in formal positions, but it also exists everywhere. To move forward with confidence and clarity in these shifting times, everyone's leadership is needed. Through its programs and activities, ALIA engages, strengthens, and builds on innate leadership capacities such as systems awareness, creativity, courage, and resilience.

ALIA leadership intensives weave together three streams: foundations in authentic leadership, skill-building for action, and community dialogue and exchange.

Visit www.aliainstitute.org to learn more.

ABOUT THE AUTHOR

Crane Wood Stookey is a Tall Ship officer and leadership coach, a professional mariner with more than 20 years experience of leadership and workforce engagement at sea. He grew up sailing traditional wooden boats on Cape Cod, Massachusetts, and the sea has been his teacher all his life.

Crane holds a US Master's license for sailing ships, and has sailed as deck officer on Tall Ships in the US and Canada. He is the founder and past director of the Nova Scotia Sea School, an award-winning experiential education and training program. He also holds a Masters of Architecture degree from Harvard and ran his own architectural practice in Boston before going to sea professionally.

Since 2006 he has been helping business and organizational leaders to bring greater effectiveness to their workforce engagement strategies and greater personal authenticity to their leadership development.

Crane was awarded the Queen's Jubilee Medal for his contribution to Canadian society.

He lives in Halifax with his wife Lesley Patten, an independent filmmaker, two cats, and his sailboat, *Prana*.

Made in the USA
Middletown, DE
15 October 2017